The Successful Novelist

A Lifetime of Lessons about Writing and Publishing

DAVID MORRELL

SOURCEBOOKS, INC.®
NAPERVILLE, ILLINOIS

This publication is designed to provide accurate and authoritative information in regard to the subject matter covered. It is sold with the understanding that the publisher is not engaged in rendering legal, accounting, or other professional service. If legal advice or other expert assistance is required, the services of a competent professional person should be sought.—*From a Declaration of Principles Jointly Adopted by a Committee of the American Bar Association and a Committee of Publishers and Associations*

A version of lesson one, "Why Do You Want To Be a Writer?" was originally published as "The Ferret Inside Me" in *Fiction Writer*, October, 1999.
A version of lesson two, "Getting Focused," was originally published as "'How Are You This Morning, David?' A Better Way to Outline" in *Fiction Writer*, April, 1999.
A version of lesson seven, "A Matter of Viewpoint," was originally published as *"First Blood*, Third Person" in *Fiction Writer*, April, 2000.
A version of lesson eleven, "What Not to Do in Dialogue," was originally published as "'He Said?' She Asked. Some Thoughts about Dialogue" in *Writing Horror*, edited by Mort Castle, published by Writer's Digest Books, 1997.
A portion of lesson fourteen, "Rambo and the Movies," was originally published as "The Man Who Created Rambo" in *Playboy*, August, 1988.
The "names" section of lesson sixteen, "Questions I'm Often Asked," was originally published in Sherrilyn Kenyon's *The Writer's Digest Character Naming Sourcebook*, published by Writer's Digest Books, 2005.

Published by Sourcebooks, Inc.
P.O. Box 4410, Naperville, Illinois 60567-4410
(630) 961-3900
Fax: (630) 961-2168
www.sourcebooks.com

Originally published in 2002 by Writer's Digest Books.

Library of Congress Cataloging-in-Publication Data

Morrell, David.
    The successful novelist : a lifetime of lessons about writing and publishing / by David Morrell.
        p. cm.
    1. Fiction—Authorship. 2. Authorship. 3. Authorship—Marketing. I. Title.

PN3365.M68 2008
808.3—dc22

                                2007027833

Printed and bound in the United States of America.

Also by David Morrell

NOVELS

First Blood (1972)
Testament (1975)
Last Reveille (1977)
The Totem (1979)
Blood Oath (1982)
The Brotherhood of the Rose (1984)
The Fraternity of the Stone (1985)
The League of Night and Fog (1987)
The Fifth Profession (1990)
The Covenant of the Flame (1991)
Assumed Identity (1993)
Desperate Measures (1994)
The Totem (Complete and Unaltered) (1994)
Extreme Denial (1996)
Double Image (1998)
Burnt Sienna (2000)
Long Lost (2002)
The Protector (2003)
Creepers (2005)
Scavenger (2007)

NOVELIZATIONS

Rambo (First Blood Part II) (1985)
Rambo III (1988)

SHORT FICTION

The Hundred-Year Christmas (1983)
Black Evening (1999)
Nightscape (2004)

ILLUSTRATED FICTION
Captain America: The End (2007)

NONFICTION
John Barth: An Introduction (1976)
Fireflies: A Father's Tale of Love and Loss (1988)
American Fiction, American Myth: Essays by Philip Young
edited by David Morrell and Sandra Spanier (2000)

Dedication

To Stirling Silliphant,
Philip Klass/William Tenn,
and John Barth,
the writers who, in chronological order,
taught me most about fiction writing

Contents

First Day of Class

෧

W hen I was seventeen, I realized that, more than anything, I wanted to be a fiction writer. I made the decision rather suddenly between 8:30 and 9:30 p.m. on the first Friday of October, 1960. How can I be so specific? Because that was when the classic TV series *Route 66* premiered. I vividly remember the power with which the show's opening sequence struck me—two hip young men in a Corvette convertible driving along a highway while a piano jazz theme pulsed and the show's title zoomed into the foreground.

At the time, I was a troubled teenager who drowsed through my high school classes (except English) and then went home to watch television until the stations went off the air at 1 a.m. My school's principal once summoned me to his office, thrust a finger at me, and announced that I'd never amount to anything. How ironic that a television program became my salvation. *Route 66* was then the main highway connecting much of the United States, so its name made a perfect title for a show about two young men who traveled the country in search of America and themselves. Their search became *my* search. I identified with the characters. (One had recently lost his father; the other had been raised in an orphanage. When I was four, my mother put me in an orphanage because she couldn't support the two of us after my father had died in World War II.) I loved the colorful "Beat" way they talked. I hung on every twist in the plots. Eager to learn everything I could about *Route 66*, I studied each episode's credits and noticed that almost every script was written by a man with the distinctive name Stirling Silliphant. The most bizarre notion took possession of me. Wouldn't it be great, I thought, to have made up all those gripping stories and to have invented that wonderful dialogue? I'd always had an abundant imagination, filled with daydreams, but this was the first time it ever occurred to me that my imagination could be productive.

A directionless seventeen-year-old boy suddenly had a purpose that he could never have dreamt of a few weeks earlier. Noticing that *Route 66* was produced by Screen Gems, a division of Columbia Pictures, I went to the local library—this was in a modest-sized city called Kitchener in Ontario, Canada—where I asked a librarian how I could find the address for Columbia Pictures. Armed with that address, I sent a handwritten letter (I didn't yet know how to type) to the mysterious Silliphant, informing him that he had inspired me to want to be a writer—that basically I wanted to be *him*.

Whatever I expected, it certainly wasn't a reply within a week, in the form of a typed, two-page, single-spaced letter in which he apologized for taking so long to get back to me. (He'd been on a boat at sea when my letter arrived, he explained.) He was flattered that I admired his work. He was delighted that he'd motivated me to try to do what *he* did. Unfortunately, he was far too busy to critique work by beginning writers. But he did offer some advice. "If you want to be a writer, the secret is to write, write, write, and keep writing," he said. "Eventually you'll find other people who want to be writers. You'll trade ideas with them. You'll critique one another's work. Keep writing. When you think you have something of merit, send it out. Chances are, the first items you submit won't be accepted, but you can't be discouraged. Keep writing. One day, if you have something of promise to say, somebody somewhere will see it and become excited and help you. It's just that simple," he concluded, "and that terribly difficult."

I never received better advice. (That letter is framed beside my desk, incidentally.) Taking a hard look at myself, I realized that desire alone wasn't going to get me anywhere–I needed to learn how to put words and stories together. I finished high school and went to college, amazing myself as much as my high school principal. My mother and stepfather worked in a furniture factory, though, and they didn't have the money for my tuition. To pay it, I had to work summers at god-awful jobs. One involved twelve-hour night shifts at a factory that made Styrofoam containers. I wore earplugs, goggles, and a mask over my nose and mouth while I shoved leftover chunks of Styrofoam into a gigantic grinder that pulverized them. The roar from the grinder (affectionately called "the snow machine") could be heard three blocks from the factory. I had a summer-long ringing in my ears and was constantly coughing up bits of plastic.

But that job was nothing compared to the one I had the *next* summer at a metal-molding factory where I made car fenders. Wearing thick gloves that became shredded by the end of each shift, I would grab a large sheet of metal, shove it into a stamping machine, press a button with my foot, cause a huge weight to come down on the metal, pull out what was now a car fender, and grab another sheet. For safety and to speed the process, my wrists were shackled to the machine so that when the weight came down, it tugged a cable that yanked my hands out of the way. One morning, the factory's personnel manager, who used to call me to his office to have literary discussions, decided to put me on a safer job. An hour later, the worker who had replaced me at the machine lost his hands when the cables failed and didn't pull him free.

I mention those jobs to emphasize my determination. Now that I knew what I wanted to be, I was prepared to do anything to make it happen. I got through those brutal summers by telling stories to myself while I worked. Although I was inspired by a screenwriter, I couldn't find any universities that offered courses in screenwriting (although these days, such courses are everywhere), so I majored in English and American literature. The then-small institution I went to (St. Jerome's College at the University of Waterloo in Canada) offered only one fiction writing course. But in retrospect, I'm glad there weren't more, because I'd have attended them all and missed various literature courses. Many of the important lessons I learned about writing fiction came from analyzing great novels. To feed my writing, I realized, I needed to read in order to discover how the experts achieved their effects.

Meanwhile, I wrote television scripts and sent them to various programs, but the scripts always came swiftly back with a note informing me that unsolicited manuscripts weren't welcome. Translation—get an agent. But how on Earth was I supposed to do that when most agents wouldn't accept writers without experience? So I wrote short stories and sent them to various magazines. Those manuscripts always came swiftly back also, accompanied with a form letter announcing something like, "Your story doesn't suit our present needs."

Eventually, I was forced to conclude that the odds against earning a living as a writer were terrible and that a day job would be a good idea. Why not get a graduate degree in American literature? I thought. Become a professor. Write fiction when I wasn't teaching. I was encouraged that Stirling Silliphant was a novelist as well as a screenwriter. So after applying to a number of doctoral programs, I went to Pennsylvania State University, where I met Philip Klass (his pen name is William Tenn), the first professional writer I'd ever talked to. Klass, who was part of the Golden Age of science fiction in the 1950s, generously put me through a crash course in technique. And with a sense of him looking encouragingly over my shoulder, in 1968 I began a novel about a disaffected Vietnam veteran named Rambo who finds himself in a private war with a small-town police chief. I called it *First Blood*.

That novel was begun eight years after the premiere of *Route 66*. I was now twenty-five. But I still wasn't confident about my writing abilities. After numerous drafts that I struggled through when I wasn't studying for classes, I decided that I'd set myself an impossible goal. I put the frustrating manuscript in a drawer and began what seemed a much more sensible project: my dissertation on the contemporary American writer John Barth. I remember a snowy night in Buffalo when Barth and I, having interrupted one of my interviews with him, were driving to a State University of

New York function that he needed to attend. Somehow he'd heard (probably from my dissertation director) that I was working on a novel. He asked me how it was going, and I replied that I'd abandoned it, that I'd finally admitted to myself that I didn't have what it took to be a published fiction writer.

That was in 1969, *nine years* after the premiere of *Route 66*. The following year I finished the dissertation, and with time on my hands before I moved to the University of Iowa to start teaching American literature, I happened across the interrupted novel. To my surprise, it somehow didn't read so badly. The next thing I knew, I was cutting and rearranging, then moving the story forward. In June of 1971, I finally finished it and sent it to an agent Philip Klass had introduced me to, Henry Morrison, but I was still so uncertain that I also sent a typescript of my dissertation.

I started teaching summer school, *finished* teaching summer school, and pretty much gave up expecting a reply when Morrison called to say that he'd sold my book. Assuming that he was talking about my dissertation, I needed a minute to realize that he meant *First Blood*, for which I would receive the lofty advance of $3,500. That wasn't going to make me rich, but then neither was being an assistant professor—my second-year salary was $13,500. The advance seemed even smaller when Morrison reminded me that I needed to pay a chunk of it in federal/state taxes, and of course an agent's fee would be deducted. But the amount I earned didn't matter as much as the fact of the sale. Eleven years after the first episode of *Route 66*, I finally became a professional writer. In my twenty-eighth year, the dream of a seventeen-year-old was fulfilled, and it happened exactly as Silliphant had said it would.

I've written millions of words since then: twenty novels, two novelizations, two books of non-fiction (not counting this one), a Christmas fable, two collections of short stories (with enough stories left over to fill a third volume), several screenplays and TV scripts, a comic book series, numerous essays and reviews as well as forewords and afterwords to books by others. To my surprise, thirty-six years have sped by. I'm in my fourth decade as a professional writer.

Although I resigned my professorship in 1986, the teacher in me remains strong and finally urged me to try yet another type of writing: *about* writing. In my long career, I accumulated a great many lessons—how to do things on the page and, equally important, how *not* to do things—a lifetime's worth of tips that I'm eager to pass along.

But please don't expect a magic formula that'll make books fall out of your head and automatically give you a wide readership. There isn't an easy way. True, on occasion a writer comes along who calculates an approach and a subject matter that turn out to be vastly popular. Nicholas Sparks (*Message in a Bottle*) is a good example. Some years ago at the *Los Angeles Times* Festival of Books, he spent a half hour with me, explaining his theory that each genre tends to have two writers who dominate it, with room for a third. For the legal thriller, there were John Grisham, Scott Turow, and the current contender. For the female private-eye novel, there were Sara Paretsky, Sue Grafton, and the current contender. You get the idea. By process of elimination, Sparks concluded that there was only *one* leader in the male romance genre, i.e., romances written by men for a female audience: Robert James Waller (*The Bridges of Madison County*). With a slot available, Sparks decided to give it a try and was vastly successful.

I don't recommend that you attempt this kind of calculation. Maintaining a career is hard to begin with but becomes even harder if you arbitrarily choose a type of fiction that happens to be currently fashionable. Let's say you take a year to write the book. It takes another year to publish the book properly. By the time your calculated effort is released, the culture you're trying to appeal to will have moved on. Interests might have changed. There's a risk that you'll be seen as irrelevant or old-fashioned. Since you can't predict how long trends will last, don't bother trying to be part of one. The only reason to write a story is that it grabs you and won't let go until you put it on paper. If there's a formula, it's based on passion and commitment. That won't guarantee a wide readership, but it *will* guarantee the satisfaction of writing a story that matters to you: the ultimate reward.

In my own case, I created one of the most recognizable characters of the late twentieth century: Rambo. But the huge commercial success that Rambo brought me was the farthest thing from my mind when I wrote *First Blood*. All I cared about was the compulsion that gripped me each day, the excitement of describing a Vietnam veteran's collision with a small-town police chief and the miniature Vietnam War that resulted. Until that time, few hardbacks had depicted that much action. My agent and I were sure that only a paperback publisher would risk accepting the book. To our surprise, a hardback publisher (M. Evans and Co., Inc.) brought it out in 1972, and just about every major newspaper and magazine reviewed it, usually favorably. Who could have figured?

The movie based on the novel faced its own obstacles. Throughout the rest of the 1970s, numerous film companies tried to adapt it but failed. That turned out to be good for the project because, after America was forced from Vietnam, angry feelings about the war meant that films with a Vietnam background wouldn't attract an audience unless they were overtly political, as was 1978's *Coming Home*. Only in 1982, when attitudes toward the war became less bitter, did *First Blood* finally reach the screen. No one associated with the production anticipated its success. Back in 1968, I couldn't possibly have predicted that Rambo would become an international phenomenon in the 1980s and 1990s. There were too many cultural variables in the future that couldn't be imagined and controlled. Don't try to outsmart the market. Just write a story you feel passionate about and do it as well as you possibly can.

With that disclaimer out of the way—there isn't any magic formula for achieving success—let's get started. The sections of this book are arranged so that they lead you through the process I follow when putting a novel or a story together, from getting the idea to focusing it, then doing the research and making the necessary choices among viewpoints and structures, then deciding what should be on that all-important first page, and so on. I'll discuss the psychology of being a fiction writer, the unique pressures and problems that face me every day. I'll use examples from my work to illustrate mistakes that I made or problems that I had trouble solving. I'll talk about Rambo and the movies, about the cultural phenomenon of the character, and about the challenges of dealing with Hollywood. I'll explain about getting published, about the business of writing, about contracts and money management. Basically, I'll try to put you in my head and teach you how I survived for so many years in this uncertain, competitive profession. For this updated edition of *Lessons from a Lifetime of Writing*, I added a major new section about publicity and marketing. I also expanded numerous portions of the original text, adding new material about topics such as what to consider when naming characters. My hope is that if you face the obstacles I encountered, you'll learn from my example how to overcome those obstacles more easily than I did, creating better fiction in the process.

Why Do You Want To Be a Writer?

When I teach at writers' conferences, I always begin by asking my students, "Why in heaven's name would you want to be writers?" They chuckle, assuming that I've made a joke. But my question is deadly sober. Writing is so difficult, requiring such discipline, that I'm amazed when someone wants to give it a try. If a student is serious about it, if that person intends to make a living at it, the commitment of time and energy is considerable. It's one of the most solitary professions. It's one of the few in which you can work on something for a year (a novel, say) with no certainty that your efforts will be accepted or that you'll get paid. On every page, confidence fights with self-doubt. Every sentence is an act of faith. Why would anybody want to do it?

The usual answer I get is, "For the satisfaction of being creative." The students nod, relieved that this troubling line of thought is over. But in fact the subject has barely been started. I rephrase my question, making it less threatening. "Why do you want to be writers?" This time I tell my students I don't want to hear about the joy of creativity. Squirms. Glances toward the ceiling or toward the floor. Someone is honest enough to say, "I'd like to earn the kind of money Stephen King does." Someone else chuckles. "Who wouldn't?" We're on our way.

Money. We're so used to hearing about the fantastic advances that writers like King, John Grisham, Tom Clancy, and Patricia Cornwell receive that many would-be writers think generous advances are the norm. The truth is that in the United States, maybe as few as twenty-five hundred fiction writers make a living at it. Every Thursday, in *USA Today*'s entertainment section, there's a list of the top fifty best-selling books. Nonfiction is grouped with fiction, hardbacks with paperbacks. Fifty books. A longer list of 150 books is available on that newspaper's website. The lowest book might have sold only a thousand copies nation-wide. Seen from this perspective, the figure of twenty-five hundred fiction writers who make a living at it seems huge. A couple of years ago, I came across an article that said the average income for a fiction writer in the United States was $6,500. I believe it. The inescapable moral, I tell my students, is that anyone who wants to become a writer had better not give up his or her day job.

"Why do you want to be writers?" I repeat. The squirms are more uncomfortable. Someone admits, not in so many words, that it would be neat to be the subject of magazine articles and to appear on the *Today* show. The writer as movie star. We go back to the usual suspects: King, Grisham, Clancy, and Cornwell (while we're at it, let's add Danielle Steele and Mary Higgins Clark—there aren't many brand names). Again, the *USA Today* list gives us perspective. Scan the names of the top fifty authors. I doubt that more than twenty will be familiar to you. Even fewer writers are famous than earn a living at it. More important, while I can't imagine anyone foolish enough to turn down money, I have trouble understanding why someone would want to be famous. As Rambo's creator, I have experience in that regard, and if your idea of a good time is to be forced to get an unlisted phone number, swear your friends to secrecy about your address, and make sure your doors are locked because of stalkers, you're welcome to it. One of my devoted fans talks to my dead mother and to the brother I never had. Another was never in the military, but having convinced himself that he's Rambo, he tried to sue me for stealing his life. In a connection I have yet to understand, he also tried to sue the governor of New York and the Order of the Raccoon, which I thought was an organization that existed only in Jackie Gleason's television show, *The Honeymooners*. Fame's dangerous, not to mention shallow and fleeting. I'm reminded of what a once-important film producer said to me before his fortunes turned for the worse: "Just remember, David. Nobody lasts forever."

In that regard, consider a travel essay that my journalist friend John Whalen once wrote for the *Washington Times* in which he described his visit to Tarzana, California. That town, twenty miles north of Los Angeles, got its name because Edgar Rice Burroughs, the creator of Tarzan, owned a ranch there. In the 1920s, Burroughs started subdividing the property into residential lots until finally the community of Tarzana was created. In a bizarre odyssey, John wandered the streets of the town, trying to find someone who knew where Burroughs had lived. "Edgar who?" and "I don't read books" were typical of the answers he received. Few people knew that Tarzana was named after Tarzan, and some didn't even know who Tarzan was. After repeated efforts, John came to a small low house concealed behind a big tree, crammed between a furniture store and a car-repair shop. The house turned out to be where Burroughs wrote his Tarzan stories. The urn containing the author's ashes was buried under the tree, but no one knew exactly where. After taking some photographs, John paused at the gate and peered back at the obscured house. "I felt very strange standing in the middle of a town named after the fictional creation of a man whose name was totally unknown to most of the people living there."

So if money and notoriety aren't acceptable answers to "Why do you want to be a writer?", and if I won't accept the easy answer, "Because of the satisfaction of being creative," what's left? My students squirm deeper into their chairs. At this point, I mention someone who seems extremely unlikely in this context: comedian/filmmaker Jerry Lewis. The students chuckle once more, assuming that this time I've definitely made a joke. But I haven't. Years ago, Jerry Lewis taught a seminar in comedy at the University of Southern California. A hot ticket. How did Jerry decide which of the many students who applied for the course actually got to attend? Did he audition them? Did he ask for tapes of their performances? Did he read printed versions of their routines? Not at all. He merely asked for an answer to the following question: "Why do you want to be a comedian?" And there was only one answer he would accept.

"Because I need to be. Because there's something in me so nagging and torturing and demanding to get out that I absolutely need to make people laugh."

Why do you want to be a writer?

Because you need to be.

My students glance up and nod, their relieved expressions saying, "Sure. Right." They have the contented look they displayed when they decided they wanted to be writers because of the satisfaction of being creative. But we're still in the land of easy answers. Do they truly understand what "need to be" means? A long time ago when I was a literature professor, a student came to my office and announced that she was going to be a writer. "When was the last time you wrote?" I asked. "Six months ago," she answered. I politely suggested that she might consider another line of work.

Writers write. It's that basic. If you just got off an assembly line in Detroit and you're certain you have the great American novel inside you, you don't grab a beer and sit in front of the TV. You write. If you're a mother of three toddlers and at the end of the day you feel like you've been spinning in a hamster cage and yet you're convinced you have a story to tell, you find a way late at night or early in the morning to sit down and write. That's a version of how Mary Higgins Clark succeeded, by the way. Because she had to. Because something inside her absolutely insisted. A half hour a day. A page a day. Whatever it takes.

Tough stuff. The profession is not for the weak-willed or for the faint of heart. But there's a payoff, and it has nothing to do with money (although it would be nice if hard work were rewarded), and it certainly has nothing to do with having your name in the newspaper. The satisfaction of being creative? Sure. But only partly and only as it relates to my next and final question: "You need to be a writer. *Why?*" This is the key to the treasure. Why do you absolutely need to be a writer? What's the source of the uneasiness that nags at you, the compulsion to spin tales and put word after word on a blank page?

That question is one of the most important challenges any would-be writer will ever need to face in his or her creative life. How honest are you prepared to be with yourself? Earlier, I mentioned that when I was a young man learning my craft, I met my first professional writer, an expert in science fiction whose pen name was William Tenn and whose real name is Philip Klass. Klass didn't like the early stories I showed him because their subject matter was familiar. They weren't any different from hundreds of other stories he'd read, he told me. The writers who go the distance, he insisted, have a distinct subject matter, a particular approach that sets them apart from everyone else. The mere mention of their names—Faulkner, for example, or Edith Wharton—conjures themes, settings, methods, tones, and attitudes that are unique to them.

How did they get to be so distinctive? By responding to who they were and the forces that made them that way. *Everyone* is unique, Klass told me. No two lives are identical. The writers who discover what sets them apart are the writers with the best chance of succeeding. "Look inside yourself," Klass said. "Find out who you are. In your case, I suspect that means find out what you're most afraid of, and that will be your subject for your life or until your fear changes." But he didn't mean fear of heights or closed spaces or fire. Those fears were merely versions of much deeper fears, he said. The fear he was talking about was like a ferret gnawing at my soul. The ferret didn't want to be caught, though. It was going to take all my honesty and introspection to find it and determine what it was.

I eventually called this method "fiction writing as self-psychoanalysis." The theory goes like this—most people become writers because they're haunted by secrets they need to tell. The writers might not know they have secrets, or if they suspect they do, they might not be sure what these mysteries are, but something in each person is bursting to get out, to be revealed. This revelation might relate to traumas that happened to the writers as adults. A lot of young men came back from the Vietnam War wanting to write novels about what they endured in combat, for example. More often, though, the secrets surround things that occurred in childhood and were never understood. To paraphrase Graham Greene, an unhappy childhood can be a gold mine for a fiction writer. Abuse comes to mind, but not necessarily sexual. Any psychological trauma, never adjusted to, can be the impetus for someone to want to be a storyteller. A contentious divorce in which one child went with mom and the other went with dad. Or a large family in which one child never got the attention that the others did. Dickens fits this theory well. After his father went to prison for failing to pay his debts, the young Dickens was taken out of school and forced to be a laborer in a squalid factory. Prisons, oppressed children, and the suffering of the poor are constants in his work.

Hemingway fits this theory, also. His prim hometown of Oak Park, Illinois, was where the saloons ended and the churches began. In his conflicted household, his mother wanted him to wear sissy clothes and play the cello while his father encouraged him to hunt, fish, and play football. His best times were summers spent at a lake in Michigan where the outdoors provided an escape from family disagreements. As soon as Hemingway was old enough, he left his repressive environment, tried to enlist as a soldier in the First World War, was turned down because of weak eyes, and finally got accepted as a Red Cross ambulance driver on the Italian front. His almost immediate duty was to pick up body parts after a massive munitions explosion. A few assignments later, he visited an Italian sentry post where an Austrian mortar killed the Italian soldiers with him and riddled him with shrapnel. While he struggled to reach cover, an enemy machine gun shot him.

The consequence of all this was that Hemingway suffered from what is now termed posttraumatic stress disorder, with symptoms that included insomnia, nightmares, and fear of the dark. But once he had sufficient distance from the war and its effect on him, his imagination returned again and again to those traumas, using them in his first mature stories and novels. From his boyhood on, Hemingway had wanted to be a writer, but his early attempts had been conventional and flat. One of his teachers, Gertrude Stein, had told him to throw it all away and start over. As soon as Hemingway confronted his nightmares, he did start over, using a tense, lean style to communicate the "grace under pressure" that his characters, like himself, struggled to achieve from their tense childhoods onward. Understanding the importance of trauma to a writer, Hemingway once advised a would-be writer to hang himself but to arrange for a friend to cut him down before he died. That way, the would-be writer would have something to put on paper.

As for my own traumas, my father (whom I never knew) died in the Second World War. As I grew up, I keenly missed the affectionate attention of a male authority figure. My feeling of abandonment was reinforced when my mother, in dire financial straits, was forced to put me in an orphanage when I was four. Eventually, she reclaimed me. Or was the woman who took me from that orphanage the same person who put me in it? Am I adopted? To provide me with a father, she remarried, but my stepfather and I didn't get along. We lived above a bar and a hamburger joint. Drunks fought under our windows. We couldn't afford a telephone, so when my mother needed to make a phone call, she went to a pay phone in the alley below. Once, a stray gunshot shattered the phone booth's window. At night, the arguments between my mother and stepfather were so severe that I fearfully put pillows under my bed covers and made them look as if I slept there. Then I crawled under the bed to sleep where I hoped I'd be protected if anyone came into my room to harm me. I made trouble at school. In grade six, I belonged to a street gang.

An objective observer would realize how disturbed my youth was. But to me, since it was the only reality I knew, my youth was normal. That's the thing about youthful traumas. Most of the time, we don't know they're extraordinary. Only when I was in my twenties did I begin to come to terms with the psychological ordeals of my youth. By then, I was writing fiction, and even when I was dramatizing a metaphoric son in conflict with a metaphoric father (*First Blood*), it was only belatedly that I understood my fascination with the topic. Fathers and sons. The theme shows up in many of my books. I'm still adjusting to the death of the father I never knew, and writing fiction is how I accomplish that—or try to. Come to think of it, the reverence I had for Stirling Silliphant and Philip Klass is close to that of a son for a father.

Consider *your* traumas, or perhaps you don't feel that you've had any. A writer friend once told me that *he* hadn't had any traumas, that his childhood was about as perfect as any child could want, until his father died. He added that comment about his father's death as an aside, something that he gave the impression that he'd gotten over. But his fiction reveals that he's still adjusting to his father's death, for in numerous books, he dramatizes an idealized version of his childhood, showing how much he longs for the perfection that ended when his father died. In a similar fashion, *you* might be unaware of how certain events in your life affected you so strongly that they compel you to want to be a writer. A better sense of the incidents that motivate you could take you farther on your way to reaching the Holy Grail of writers: a subject matter that's your own.

How do you discover what those traumas and that subject matter are? Here's an exercise that I've found to be helpful. People often ask me where my story ideas come from. Repeating a joke by Stephen King, I answer that there's a company in Cleveland or some such place. It's called the Writers Idea Shop, and the first of every month, it sends me a box of ideas. This usually gets a laugh, after which I say that, actually, ideas swarm around me all the time—from newspapers, magazines, and television, from casual comments that my wife makes, from things my cat does, whatever. This is partially true. But it's a simple answer to a complex question, and only if I feel that the person I'm talking to has the time and is receptive, do I say the following.

My ideas don't come from outside. They come from within— from my daydreams. I'm not referring to the type of daydream that you consciously create: deliberately imagining how wonderful it would be to achieve a coveted goal, for example. Instead, I mean the type of daydream that comes to you spontaneously, an unbidden message from your subconscious. Basically, the deepest part of you is sending a story to the surface. Pay attention. The primal author in you is at work.

Daydreams come in two types: attractive and repelling. You're at a business meeting or you're driving the kids to school, and all of a sudden, in your imagination, you're on the beach at Cancun. No surprise there. You're bored with what you're doing. Your subconscious transported you to a pleasurable experience. Note how I phrased that statement. Out of boredom, *you* didn't transport yourself. Your subconscious did. You had no control over it. You could strain your imagination all day and still not create as total and sensual an experience as your subconscious did. You don't just see that beach. You hear the waves splashing. You feel the sand beneath you, the heat of the sun on your skin, and the tickle of the breeze in your nostrils. You taste the salt on the rim of your margarita. You smell the sweetness of an approaching afternoon rain shower. It's not like watching a movie in your mind. A movie is apart from you, on a flat screen, presenting only images and sound. *This* is a three-dimensional imaginary experience that totally envelopes you, engaging all your physical senses.

Now let's talk about the other kind of daydream—the repellent one. You're at a business meeting or you're driving the kids to school, and suddenly, in your imagination, as vividly as in the Cancun experience, you're trapped in a terrifying wide-awake nightmare. Interestingly, while most of us would agree that lying on the beach at a luxury resort is a situation we'd like to be in, we don't have the same consensus when it comes to what terrifies us. I have a friend with a phobia about snakes, for example. In contrast, I find snakes kind of interesting. Another friend doesn't like closed spaces whereas they don't bother me a bit. Other things scare me a lot, though. All you need to do is read my fiction to find out what they are.

Consider the implications. It's understandable why the subconscious would transport us from boring, real-life situations into pleasurable fantasies. But why on Earth does the subconscious sometimes transport us from those same boring, real-life situations into fantasies that are terrifying? From one point of view, the mechanism doesn't make sense. From another point of view, though, it makes all kinds of sense, and it parallels my question to my students: "Why do you want to be writers?" Why do you have spontaneous wide-awake nightmares? And what is the principle of selection by which your subconscious terrifies you in one way while *my* subconscious terrifies me in another?

We're at the heart of the issue. The difference between fiction writers and civilians is that we make it our life's work to put our daydreams and day-nightmares on paper. Most of the time we don't understand the secrets and demons that our spontaneous imaginings contain. All we feel is that there's something in us demanding to be released in the form of a story. Philip Klass told me, "What you fear is like a ferret gnawing at your soul. The more you try to catch it, the more it tries to hide. You'll only get hints and guesses of what and where it is." To this, I add: Day-nightmares are messages from your subconscious, hinting to you what that ferret is about. They're disguised versions of your secret. They're metaphors for why you want to be a writer.

The breakthrough I had as a writer came one hot August afternoon when I was twenty-five. I'd been writing tired conventional fiction for so long that I was in creative despair. I desperately wanted to be a writer, but I had no idea why I felt that way or what I wanted to write about. At the end of my creative resources, I gave up—and immediately had the most intense, wide-awake nightmare I'd ever experienced. I was making my way through a sweltering forest. Bushes crowded me. Sweat rolled down my face. I heard noises behind me. At first, I assumed that a squirrel was rooting for something in the underbrush. But as the sporadic crinkle of leaves sounded closer, the sound seemed more and more like cautious footsteps. Someone was in the forest with me.

Someone was creeping up on me. I can't express how vividly I felt that I was actually in that forest—and how fearfully certain I was that someone intended to kill me. As abruptly as it came, the multisensory illusion ended. It was as if I'd had an out-of-body experience. Suddenly, I found myself staring not at a forest but at my desk and the typewriter on it, a blank sheet of paper taunting me. I'd never experienced any other daydream as powerfully. I didn't understand the process, but I was sure of one thing: I wanted to know what happened next. Thus I began my first true David Morrell short story.

Ever since that long-ago afternoon, I trained myself to pay attention to my daydreams/nightmares, to be aware of them as they're happening, to wonder why certain imaginary situations are so insistent, and to use the most compelling of them as the inspiration for novels and short stories. After the fact, I learned to realize how the plots that attract me are metaphors for my psyche. That story about a man being hunted in a forest dramatizes the helplessness I felt at that time. What was hunting me? Time, ambition, frustration—name it. In the story, the hero (me) survived by overcoming his fear and maintaining control, a theme that is constant in my work. Another constant theme shows up in my novel *The Brotherhood of the Rose*. There, two orphans are trained by a surrogate father to be killers for a rogue intelligence agency. They don't kill for money or politics. They do it for love. And when the surrogate father turns against them in order to protect himself, they set out in a fury to get even. Freudian as can be. But I wrote the entire novel before I realized why my subconscious would have compelled me to write about orphans and fathers. The plot was a disguised version of the story of my life.

I want to emphasize the word "disguised." I'm not suggesting that you write stories that explicitly address your psychological concerns. That would be tedious and mechanical. Plots are at their best when they serve as metaphors for, and not explicit descriptions of, their author's psychological state. That's what daydreams are: disguises. More often than not, the author can't see through them. All the writer knows is that the story insisted on being told, that his or her imagination wouldn't rest until the images and characters that haunted it were brought into the light. The best stories choose us. We don't choose them.

I think that the *type* of stories we tell also chooses us. I referred to Stephen King a couple of times. Might as well do it again. Critics often ask him (their tone is sniffingly aloof) why he writes horror. King's response is, "What makes you think I have a choice?" Exactly. In his book *On Writing*, King describes the brutal poverty of his childhood and the twelve miles he hitchhiked each Saturday to a movie theater that specialized in horror movies, which provided a distraction from his poverty. The horror novels, stories, and comic books he compulsively read fulfilled the same function. Made-up horror helped him temporarily forget the burdens of life. Is it any surprise that his urge to write led him to tell the kind of stories that gave him relief when he was a boy?

A similar urge led me to write thrillers. When I was a kid, the family arguments drove me from our apartment above the hamburger joint. I went to a crowded bus stop, where I asked someone to give me a nickel. "Mister, I lost my bus fare." A nickel is what it cost to get a ride on the bus, but fifteen cents is what it cost to get into a movie, which was my goal. So when everybody got on the bus, I hung back and went to another bus stop, where I again begged for a nickel. If the bus stops didn't get me enough money, I waited outside bars, hoping that drunks would lose coins as they came outside, trying to pocket their money. Often my patience was rewarded. When I finally had my fifteen cents, I then had to beg an adult going into the movie theater to buy a ticket for me (I was only ten, and because it was after dark, I couldn't get into the theater by myself). I always picked a young couple who didn't have wedding rings. "Mister, will you please pretend I'm your kid and buy my ticket for me? I promise you'll never see me again when we're inside." The reason I picked unmarried couples was that the woman would look at the man to see how he reacted to a child's request (that is, what kind of father would this guy be?). Sensing that he was being tested, each man always bought my ticket.

So finally, I was in the theater, which in those days looked like a palace and where I was safe from the family arguments, escaping into the movie on the screen. The films that made the most impression on me were Hitchcock-type thrillers. So is it any wonder that the stories I love to tell are the kind that gave me an escape when I was a kid? And is it any wonder that the fan letters I most treasure are from readers trying to cope with a personal disaster? A divorce, a fire, a flood, a crippling car accident, a loved one's death, the loss of a job—name the worst thing that happened to you. People trying to survive these things write to thank me for distracting them from their pain, just as I was distracted in that movie theater when I was a troubled child.

Apply this mechanism to yourself. Perhaps you want to write romances or science fiction or mainstream novels. Unlike many critics, I make no distinction in terms of whether any type of fiction is more worthy than any other type. They all offer opportunities for imagination and verbal skills. In this regard, Peter Straub is a model. He wrote *Ghost Story* and *Mystery* with such respect, bringing to those genres such literary honesty, that he showed us the essence of what a ghost story and a mystery are. Any type of story is only a means—what a writer does with it is what matters. You'll find it revealing if, after asking yourself "Why do I want to be a writer?", you ask yourself, "Why do I want to write this particular kind of fiction?"

"Because I need to."

"Why do you need to?"

If you follow the logic in the progression of these questions, if you pay attention to the ferret that's gnawing inside you, you'll have a subject matter that's your own. You'll also approach your favorite type of story in a way that has special meaning to you. You'll be an original and not an imitator. Because you're true to yourself. Because you use your unique one-of-a-kind psyche as your guide. It may be that you'll never be one of those twenty-five hundred writers who earn a living at it. But that was never the point in the first place. You didn't become a writer to make money. You became a writer because your ferret and your daydreams/nightmares forced you to. If you do achieve financial success, all the better. But in the meantime, you did what you knew you must, and your reward was—only now is it a valid answer—the satisfaction of self-expression, of being creative.

Getting Focused

An idea for a story has taken control of you, and you're eager to put it on the page. What happens next? I know of few occasions in which a story came to a writer perfectly formed. Most of the time, your idea needs to be focused. You need to make decisions about characters, setting, viewpoint, and so on. How do you go about this? Some fiction writing instructors recommend plot outlines, but I find outlines restricting and prefer an unconventional alternative: a written conversation with myself that's easy to do and stimulates my imagination.

The liability of plot outlines is that they're time consuming to produce and tedious to read. One day you have a daydream or you open the newspaper, and something gives you an idea for a novel. A tenth of an idea, really. A hundredth of one. You think about it while you take a shower, walk the dog, or get stuck in traffic. A few additions to the plot occur to you. Day by day, you continue the process, going about your routine while slowly developing your idea. Who's the main character? What's the setting? You talk about the project with a friend, a spouse, or whomever. The conversations help to focus what you want to do and lead you toward further turning points in the story. Often you're not even aware that you're thinking about the plot. Your subconscious is doing the work.

Finally the idea coheres, so you sit down to write an outline. Or maybe, a little like working on a jigsaw puzzle, you put each plot development on paper as it occurs to you. Either way, when the outline is completed, you try to be objective about it, and . . . well, let's face it, outlines are discouragingly dull. Some formats even use subcategories along with large- and small-caps letters and Roman numerals, making the document resemble a corporate report.

CHAPTER ONE

A. Marion wakes up one morning and discovers that her husband hasn't come home from a business dinner the previous evening.
   a. She phones the executive who organized the dinner and learns
      i.   that her husband left the restaurant at ten o'clock.
      ii. that he seemed preoccupied throughout the dinner.
      iii. that he consumed more alcohol than was usual for him.
   b. She phones the police to find out if he was in an accident.
      i.   They don't have any information about him.
   c. She phones the hospitals in the area.
      i.   Same answer.
   d. She phones her best friend to get advice about what to do.

And so on. My format might seem exaggerated, but I have actually seen many outlines that look like this. Even those that use standard paragraphs often read as if they were structured in the above manner. Reduced to essentials, the majority of plot summaries will put you to sleep. To be interesting, plots require dramatization, but for many beginning writers, the completion of the outline has been so major a goal that it's hard to muster the energy to approach the far more daunting objective of starting the book.

Moreover, it's difficult to overcome the insecurity that an outline can create. By now you're so familiar with the story that you begin to wonder whether it's as interesting as you first thought. Except for the most confident and determined writer, familiarity breeds contempt. All those isolated moments of inspiration that excited you, all the intriguing possibilities that the initial hundredth of a notion promised—what have you got to show for them? A bland chronology. At this point, many potentially good books have gone unwritten, or if they do get written, their authors sometimes obsessively conform to the outlines (after all, a lot of time went into it) with the result that the books feel as mechanical as the outlines did.

What's to be done? For starters, let's identify the inadequacies of the process I just described. One limitation would be that a plot outline puts too much emphasis on the surface of events and not enough on their thematic and emotional significance. As a consequence, the book that results from the outline sometimes feels thin and mechanical. Another limitation would be that an outline doesn't provide a step-by-step record of the psychological process that you went through to work out the story. It only documents the final result. As a consequence, if you become too familiar with the story and lose interest in it, you have difficulty re-creating your initial enthusiasm. Still a further problem relates to those conversations you had with your friends or your significant other. Hemingway insisted that a writer shouldn't talk about a story before it was written. He felt that too many good ideas ended in the air rather than on the page and, worse, that the emotional release of talking about a story took away the pressure of needing to write it.

Writing. That's the point. While all this thinking and talking has been going on, not a lot of writing has been accomplished. But a writer, like a concert pianist, has to keep in daily practice. The ability to write is a perishable skill. I learned this the hard way in 1995 when, after a long project called *Extreme Denial* had left me exhausted, I took a couple of weeks off. At least, that was my intention, but the weeks stretched into an entire summer. When I finally came back to my desk, I discovered that my hard-earned skills had atrophied. My sentences were flabby. My scenes lacked focus. My dialogue wandered. With great effort, I was forced to retrain myself. I took from that experience a resolve that, even when I didn't have a project, I still needed to spend a portion of each day at my desk, performing the equivalent of a pianist's exercises.

What I'm about to propose is such an exercise. Instead of waiting to write until you've thought through an idea, why not write *as* you think? The format is a conversation with yourself, and it avoids the problems I mentioned earlier. It encourages you to delve below the surfaces of a conventional outline so that a richer book has the potential to be written. It provides a record of the psychological process by which you worked out the story, and thus, if overfamiliarity causes you to lose your enthusiasm for the story, all you need to do is reread the document and reacquaint yourself with the chain of thought that made you excited in the first place. Further, it allows you to have a conversation about the story without the risk of your best ideas ending in the air or of your conversation providing a release that takes away the pressure to write, for in this case the conversation occurs *as* you write, and the person you're talking to is your alter ego.

The idea for this method came to me a long time ago when I watched a television interview with Harold Robbins, who was then at the height of his bestselling fame. The interviewer asked Robbins if he had any rituals that helped him start writing each day. Did he make coffee or sharpen a lot of pencils or whatever? Yes, Robbins said, he talked to his typewriter. He thought of it as a compilation of his audience, and he imagined that he had an affectionate relationship with it. He even gave the typewriter a human name, let's say Jennifer. Thus each day he sat down and mentally asked, "How are you today, Jennifer?"

In his imagination, the typewriter's female voice replied, "Wonderful, and how are *you* this morning, Harold?"

"Great," he said, "I can't wait to get on with the story I was telling you yesterday."

"Yes, it was awfully exciting," the typewriter said, "and I'm eager as can be to know what happens next."

What appealed to me about this dialogue wasn't the notion of casting a typewriter as an admiration society, although there are worse ways to boost one's confidence. Rather, I saw this dialogue as an opportunity to work out a story in a way that amounts to a form of self-psychoanalysis. Let's go back to that moment when a daydream or an article in a newspaper so engages you that you start thinking it would make a good basis for a novel. At this point, instead of meditating while you shower or walk the dog or get stuck in traffic, you head for your desk and write while meditating. You make a record of your thoughts while you're thinking them.

"How are you this morning, David?"

"Great! I just had a wonderful idea for a story."

"Fabulous! Tell me about it. What's the idea?"

Now remember, you're writing all this. You're not staring out the window. You're doing a finger exercise (continuing the metaphor of music) that will soon prompt you to start composing: because you need to answer the question, "What's the idea?"

With me, the initial attempt at an answer wanders all over the place. The following actually happened. "Well," I wrote to my word processor, "I read an article in *Architectural Digest*, and something about it really intrigued me. In the nineteen-twenties, Frank Lloyd Wright's son designed a house for a movie star named Ramon Novarro. It's up in the Hollywood Hills, and it's one of the most striking houses I've ever seen."

At this point, I ran out of words. I needed to prime myself. Staring down at my keyboard, I typed what many of you are probably thinking about the above paragraph. "So what?"

Use those two words a lot. They'll compel you to start analyzing and developing, as they did me. In typical fashion, my response was one of uncertainty. "I'm not sure *what* the idea is. I just found that art-deco house so captivating. I'd like to write about it."

"Why?"

Use *that* word a lot, also. It leads you to the moment of truth. If you don't have an answer, you'll never be able to write a story about whatever glimmer of an idea you had. Why I find a particular idea interesting is for me the major hurdle that I need to get over before I can start to create a plot. I'm not a fast writer. It takes me anywhere from one to two years to write a novel. I begin the project with great excitement, but by the time I get to page 100, I feel less energetic. I'm too close to the material. I look ahead, realize that I've got a long way to go, and start to fear that my monumental effort might not be worth the result. The film director Francois Truffaut once said that making a movie is like getting into a stagecoach. At first, you're hoping for a pleasant ride. After a while, you're praying you'll get out in one piece. I've often felt that the same goes for writing a novel. So when I start a project, I use this method as a way of making sure that the idea interests me enough to carry me through the various psychological perils of composition.

"Why does that house interest you, David?"

"I'm not sure."

"That's not good enough. You're going to be sitting here for a couple of hours. You might as well try as hard as you can to get inside the idea. Why does the house interest you?"

"Well, maybe it's because the photographs of the house show that, even though it's in the Hollywood Hills, there aren't any houses around it. There aren't even any shrubs. In the photographs, the hills are totally barren except for the house."

I left that paragraph in rough shape to emphasize that the style of this focusing technique is truly conversational. I'm not worried about style at this point. I want a stream-of-consciousness feeling but with conventional punctuation and syntax. The sentences should be complete, but they need not be polished. I want the idea to carry me forward, so I resist the urge to go back and fix a sentence. When I reread, I correct spelling, but otherwise, unless a sentence is totally incomprehensible, I leave it alone. I want to be loose. I want to be an instrument to the idea.

"So, in the photos, there aren't any houses or shrubs around the house. So what?" (Again that important question.)

"Well, it's kind of eerie when I consider that the same area today is crammed with houses and trees and cars. I wonder if the house still exists. I wonder what it looks like now. It's too bad *Architectural Digest* didn't include photos of the area today. It would be interesting to compare the two."

"Why?"

I keep asking that question. Every time I get to a point where the idea seems to sputter to a halt, I prime myself with why, why, why.

"Why would it be interesting to compare the photographs, David?"

"To see the difference between then and now."

"So the article appealed to you because it subconsciously made you aware of the difference between the past and the present?"

"I guess so."

"That's not good enough. Give me a decent answer."

"Yeah, it's something about the past and the present. That movie star is dead now, but there he is in the photographs, sitting on his fabulous patio. He's dust in a coffin, but he's still alive in the photos. They're chilling."

"It sounds like you're as interested in the photographs as you are in the house."

"I guess that's true. I've always had a morbid reaction to photographs. When I look at family albums, I'm struck by the contradiction that so many of the people in those photos are dead and yet they look so alive."

I've come a long way from the house, but I'll go farther. What first interested me leads me in unexpected directions. One facet of my mind is questioning the other, leading it toward moments of personal truth that will soon be translated into a narrative. The project I'm preparing will have personal relevance, my feelings about the past and death. It will be a process of self-discovery. I can't imagine spending a year or more on a novel and not emerging from it with greater self-awareness than when I began. That way, even if the project doesn't attract a publisher, my time has been well spent.

"How do you write a novel about photographs, David?"

"Maybe my main character is a photographer."

"But you write thrillers. How are you going to get a photographer into all the action you'll need to invent? How can you make him believably survive all the danger? He'll need a tough background."

"Maybe he was a war photographer. He's used to being shot at and having explosions go off near him."

"That could work."

"Maybe something happened to him while he was photographing a war. Maybe he decided to change the focus of his career. Maybe he became an artistic photographer to document hope instead of despair."

Note that one item led to another and another until suddenly I'm talking about characterization and theme. Before I know it, I ask myself for the character's name and how old he is and what he looks like, and the story continues to grow. After a couple of hours, I reach a point where inspiration flags, so I quit, let my subconscious work on the idea, and go play tennis or check for tomato worms in the vegetable garden. The next time I return to my desk, I'm excited to see how much farther I'll be able to develop the idea. I reread what I've written. I don't do any editing. I simply go through the material as a record of my flowing thoughts, and then I start writing again. In a written conversation with yourself, there is seldom a case of writer's block. There are too many ways to break it.

"How are you this morning, David?"

"Okay, I guess."

"That's not a rousing affirmative. What's the matter?"

"Well, I was looking forward to rereading this material, but now that I have, I'm disappointed. It's not as good as it felt yesterday."

"Why? Don't tell me you lost your interest in the idea."

"No. Something in it continues to haunt me. But I haven't got there yet."

"Well, let's take it a step at a time. What in the material you wrote yesterday doesn't seem effective?"

"For starters, I was excited about a Lloyd Wright house that belonged to a movie star in the nineteen-twenties, but all of a sudden, I'm planning a novel about a photographer. I'm all over the place."

"Not necessarily. Maybe you can connect them. Maybe the photographer takes pictures of the house. Maybe he wants to buy it. What's it look like inside?"

"There are pictures of the interior in *Architectural Digest*. The rooms have chrome art-deco furniture from the twenties. The dining-room walls have strings of black beads. Weird. But that was then. The interior would be different now."

"Not necessarily. What if it hasn't changed?

"A house from the twenties with an interior that remains the same? The past and the present overlapping?"

And so on. I keep raising questions and answering them. I don't stick to an agenda but instead roam all over the place. I pick up and set down ideas. I go away. I come back. If I seem to exhaust one direction, I have plenty of others to explore. For example, what war was my photographer in? (Bosnia.) What caused his career crisis? (Bones from hundreds of corpses in a mass grave being pulverized by a tree shredder.) I keep prompting myself. I keep asking who, what, when, and how, but most of all "So what?" and "Why, why, why?" Eventually I connect the dots and discover that I have not only a plot but also characters whose issues are important to me; in other words, a theme. Meanwhile if I get distracted or inspiration fails, all I need to do is reread my conversation with myself and I'll be forced back into my chain of thought.

Somewhere along the line, I'll also need to question myself about the techniques I'm going to use. What's the best viewpoint for this story? Will the first person work here, or is it better to use third person limited, or do I want to switch among characters in an omniscient way? What scene provides the strongest, most logical way of beginning the story? How am I going to avoid flashbacks? What sort of structure do I want? (Since my hero was a photographer, I made the controversial decision to structure the novel so that two plots overlapped in what I hoped would be a novelistic equivalent of a photographic double exposure.) I debate these and similar technical matters just as I debate elements of the plot. I do it in writing. You'll be amazed how many time-wasting errors you avoid.

The above process is how I developed a novel called *Double Image*, which is about a former war photographer who so admires an old house that he buys it. There, he discovers a trove of photographs taken in 1933, all depicting the same beautiful woman. The odds are that the woman is now dead, and yet she looks so alive in the photos that my hero becomes obsessed with her and sets out to learn everything he can about her. The overall theme is that the present (the hero's war trauma) has so devastated him that he's desperate to escape into the past. His life is a double exposure. At one point, he comes across photographs of Los Angeles in the 1920s and tries to find the exact spots where the photographer took the pictures so long ago. He then takes new pictures, trying to merge the past and the present.

The written conversation that allowed me to focus my imagination took me several weeks to write and amounted to twenty single-spaced pages. One day, I discovered that the questions my alter ego kept asking me had become so refined that I was two pages into the first chapter before I realized that I had actually started the book. Half a year later, in the dark days of composition, I was awfully glad to have the written conversation with myself to remind me of where I had been and where I was going.

This format is so loose and easy to do that you can handily modify it to your own requirements. You don't need the quotation marks, and it may be that once you get used to questioning yourself you won't need the "How are you this morning, David?" preamble. There's no reason you can't jump to "I saw something on the street today, and it got me thinking." But what I like about "How are you this morning, David?" is that even if you don't have a thought in your head, at least you're writing.

Remember to keep asking the most important questions: "Why is this idea interesting to me? Why would I want to spend a year or more working on it?" As you proceed in your self-analytic quest to create a story, you'll learn as much about yourself as you do about your work, growing as a person as well as a writer.

At the end of this creative exercise, you can arrange the wandering thoughts of your conversation with yourself and turn them into a plot summary that you can submit to an agent or an editor. But before you can summarize your plot, you need to have one, and understanding the nature of plot is the subject of our next session.

Plot

The following situation happens to all professional fiction writers. For some reason, it takes place more often at cocktail parties or on crowded airplanes. Someone you don't know, an absolute stranger, turns to you and asks, "So what do *you* do?" This isn't quite as rude as wanting to know how much money you earn, but it's in that realm. In some rough areas where I've done research, the question "So what do *you* do?" can get you put in the hospital. But in the situation I'm describing, an evasive answer such as "I'm in business" or "I do this and that" leads to further questions, such as "What kind of business?" or "What do you mean by 'this and that'?" Short of being antisocial, there's no way around the problem. You need to give a specific answer.

As you'll see, I'm not being uppity or difficult here, because if you're a fiction writer, at all costs you do not want to give a truthful answer.

"So what do *you* do?"

My favorite answer is a half-truth: "I'm a literature professor." It's an occupation I know enough about to give further answers if pressed. Plus, hardly anybody, not even students, wants to talk to a literature professor. Follow my example and refer to your day job.

Why do I feel so strongly about this evasion? Watch how the conversation proceeds.

"So what do *you* do?"

Can't keep it to yourself. Faint touch of pride. "I'm a fiction writer."

"Oh." Long pause. Glances down at the floor. Thoughtful nod. Glances up at the ceiling. Pensive expression. "I don't suppose . . ."

Looks directly at you. Pained narrowing of eyebrows. "I wonder if . . ." Tortured movement of the head from side to side. "Is it possible I've read anything of yours?"

Now you're stuck. Now you need to mention the book you wrote, and this is the answer you get: "Gosh, I must have missed that one."

This is a universal fact of life. There's something about this situation that brings predictable forces together. Even if you're on the bestseller list, I'll bet the price of your book that the questioner has never read a word of what you've written and has definitely never heard of you.

To test this truth, I have sometimes opened myself to disdain by answering, "You might know something I've written—*First Blood*."

"*First Blood*? What's *that* about?"

It's sometimes easier to refer to the movie, but a lot of people erroneously think that its title is *Rambo*, so if I want to compound my foolishness by trying to be honest, I say, "It's a novel that became a movie about a Vietnam veteran named Rambo."

"*Who?*"

"Rambo."

Giving me a look of pity. "Gosh, I must have missed that one."

I'm not exaggerating. Testing my theory, I have gone through this conversation more times than my self-esteem can stand. If I'd written *Moby Dick*, *War and Peace*, or *The Catcher in the Rye*, the answer would be identical in this situation. Keep remembering what I said about fame being a lousy reason to want to be a writer.

"So what do *you* do?"

"I'm a literature professor."

"Oh."

And that'll be the end of that.

But let's say you're masochistic enough to be honest. The conversation gets worse.

"Gosh, I must have missed that one. You know, when I retire from medicine (the law, big business), I'm going to write a novel."

I applaud the intention, but the truth is that no writing will ever get done. The assumption here is that writing a novel is so easy anyone can do it if only there weren't the pressures of an important busy schedule, which apparently you, dear writer, do not have— otherwise you wouldn't be screwing around, sitting at a keyboard or notepad, making up stories. In fact, a good story often reads so easily that civilians seem to think that the darn things write themselves. Whenever I leave the house, I make sure that one of my novels is hard at work. I expect five pages by the time I get back.

But we still haven't reached the end of this situation. This is its climax, and it brings me to my point. When the person you're talking to claims to have a great idea for a novel, set down your drink and flee, or if you're on an airplane, tell your questioner that you absolutely need to go to the bathroom. Otherwise, you won't like what comes next.

"In fact, it's such a great idea I'm sure it'll be a bestseller and make a hit movie," the person says. "The problem is, I just don't have the time to actually write it. I wish I could find somebody to do it for me. You don't know any bestselling authors looking for ideas, do you? I'd be glad to split the money fifty-fifty. What about *you*? Are *you* busy? Maybe *you* could use this great idea and write it for me."

"Sorry. I've got several projects I'm trying to finish and—"

"It wouldn't take much work. You could write it in your spare time. Honestly, it's such a great idea, it'll probably write itself."

Now let's test how dumb we are. Do we dare ask, "What's the idea?"

I'm reminded of a novelist/screenwriter friend who lived in New York and was summoned urgently to Los Angeles by a movie studio whose supreme commander had an idea for a sure-fire, no-doubt-about-it blockbuster film. So hot was this idea, the executive wouldn't tell it to the writer over the phone. For security reasons, the revelation had to be done in person. Thus my friend flew all the way across the continent and drove to the executive's office, where the executive worked the combination on an office safe and removed a sheet of paper, which he reverentially handed over with the awe of Moses coming down from the mountain.

These are the two words my friend stared at:

Biological weapons.

"Biological weapons?"

"Yeah, isn't that a great idea? It shouldn't take you long to deliver the script. I've done most of the hard work. Go off and write it."

"Biological weapons" is a version of what the questioner at the party or on the plane is going to say. It's like those one-line descriptions of television shows and movies listed in the newspaper. "A mad man tries to poison New York's water supply." "A woman with a brain tumor tries to make peace with her estranged children before she dies." "Uncle Joe has trouble changing a tire."

These one-liners are situations. Topics. Skinny ones. Vague and unfocused. Everyone has them. A civilian's dog and cat get along so well that the owner says, "Somebody ought to do a book (movie) about them." A civilian reads a newspaper article about a plane crash. A young man and woman survived and somehow stayed alive on a snow-drifted mountain for three weeks. Strangers when they met, they got married after they were rescued. "Somebody ought to do a book (movie) about that."

But neither situation is a plot. There's a huge difference between having an "idea" and elaborating it into a plot. People understood this distinction until the early 1980s, when a shift in the movie industry made situations seem all-important. Prior to then, directors ruled Hollywood. But creative enthusiasm sometimes led to out-of-control budgets and pictures that weren't mainstream enough to earn a profit. As a consequence, one studio, Paramount, started a trend by deciding that producers should be the controlling force. The executives who made this decision began their careers in television, where producers have the authority and everyone else follows orders. They wanted to apply this approach to the movie business.

One other executive, the villain of this trend, had no experience in television and little in the movies. He was a cocaine addict named Don Simpson, who used his charismatic personality to talk his way quickly up through the ranks until, in 1981, he became president of Paramount Productions. There, he invented terms such as "tentpole" and "event" to describe big-budget summer movies that had a must-see feel to them. What made them "must-see"? Their "high concept," another term that Simpson is said to have invented.

High concept refers to an intriguing one-line description of a story. Thus *Alien* is a "haunted house in deep space." *Titanic* is "Romeo and Juliet on a sinking ship." *Gladiator* is "unjustly perse-cuted Roman general becomes a gladiator, gets to wear a skirt, and saves Rome." The purpose of high concept is to reduce a story to its simplest level and then to make sure that this simple reduction has some punch to it. Simpson took the theory of high concept to such an extreme that, with his attention span compromised by drugs and alcohol, he didn't want to hear the plot of a proposed film. All he wanted was a thirty-second "pitch."

"What's this thing called?"

"*Moby Dick.*"

"Get to the point. I've got drugs to take. What's the hook?"

"A one-legged captain chases a white whale."

Takes a snort of cocaine. "That's the stupidest idea I ever heard." Takes another snort of cocaine.

That imagined conversation is reportedly not far from what actually happened. See Charles Fleming's disturbing biography of Simpson, *High Concept.* One trouble with this approach is that many great plots are too complicated to be reduced to a couple of words (*Moby Dick* being one of them). As a consequence, in the age of high concept they're less likely to attract a studio's attention. Another trouble is that producers eventually want a plot that exactly matches the high concept, that is, one that's dumbed down until there's no subtlety or complexity whatsoever.

A glance at the films that Simpson and his partner Jerry Bruckheimer produced illustrates the point. *Flashdance*, *Beverly Hills Cop*, *Top Gun*, *Days of Thunder*, and *The Rock*, to mention a few. Here are their high concepts. Female welder performs sweaty artistic dances in bars. Black cop from Detroit fights crime in Beverly Hills. Tom Cruise in a fighter jet. Tom Cruise in a race car. Escapee from Alcatraz breaks into it. Apart from their weirdness when summarized, these films have two things in common. They have quick, often incomprehensible MTV-type cutting. And they're loud. Most of them also have a lot of pulsing songs that producer Julia Phillips called "sound tracks in search of movies."

High concept eventually corrupted the book business as much as it did the movies. During the 1990s, many editors began to use high concept as a way of judging the marketability of books. Could the plot be summarized in a catchy sentence? Was there a few-word hook that could be used on the cover and in ads? It's hard enough to invent an interesting, meaningful plot without being forced to choose one that can be summarized in a compelling sentence. Marketing was once not an author's respon-sibility. Now, more and more, with downsizing in publishing, authors are expected to be unofficial members of the marketing department and supply a hook.

As a result, some authors are tempted to contrive a plot that's controlled by an arbitrary concept and sacrifices character in favor of mechanical twists and turns.

"A serial-killer novel? Hey, I can give you all the serial killers you want. That has-been on the bestseller list has only three serial killers in his novel. I'm much more creative than that. I can give you *five*. All in one book. It's *Oliver Twist* crossed with *The Silence of the Lambs*. It's all about a *school* for serial killers, and . . ."

Resist the temptation. Once you fall into the trap of high concept, it's hard to escape. You might be financially successful in the short run, but in the long run your career will suffer as will, secretly, your self-esteem. You'll turn into that movie executive who thinks that coming up with a sensational topic (biological weapons) makes him a writer.

Plot. That's what counts. Let's discuss what the word means. For me, the best analysis comes from a series of lectures that E. M. Forster (*A Passage to India*) delivered at Trinity College, Cambridge, in 1927. These lectures were eventually collected in a book called *Aspects of the Novel*. A story, Forster says, is based on the progression of time. This happened, and then this happened, and then this happened. It's the kind of summary that people in a hurry sometimes provide about a book or a film. "The king died and then the queen died" is Forster's famous example of a story.

A plot, though, is a more sophisticated form of narrative and is based on causality. "The king died, and then the queen died of grief." If you look closely at that statement, you discover that at heart it suggests a mystery. Indeed, according to Forster, *all* good plots are mysteries. I love this notion because it supports my belief that there are no inferior types of fiction, only inferior practitioners of them. This is Forster's rationale:

> "The queen died, no one knew why, until it was discovered that it was through grief at the death of the king." This is a plot with a mystery in it, a form capable of high development ... Consider the death of the queen. If it is in a story we say "and then?" If it is in a plot we ask "why?" That is the fundamental difference between these two aspects of the novel. A plot cannot be told to a gaping audience of cave-men or to a tyrannical sultan or to their modern descendent the movie public. They can only be kept awake by "and then—and then—" They can only supply curiosity. But a plot demands intelligence and memory also.

Why, why, why. That is the metaphoric mystery in your novel. As you develop your plot in your written conversation with yourself, keep asking yourself why your characters are doing what you want them to or, better, why your characters are doing what *they* want to. In a lifelike novel, your characters will sometimes refuse to participate in a scene you constructed. They'll freeze. So will the scene. Like Method-trained actors, the characters will insist on knowing their motivation, their *true* motivation, for the paces you're trying to force them through do not feel right. A revolt by your characters might sound odd until it happens to you. When it does, congratulate yourself. You'll have reached a new level of fiction writing skill, the ability to distinguish bogus scenes from authentic ones. Almost always, you can unfreeze a scene by pretending to be the most stubborn character and asking, "What in blazes is my true motivation?"

Plot and character. You can't have one without the other. In the worst kind of novel (high concept), the plot controls the characters, often forcing them to do ridiculous things because, at any narrative cost, the novelist must strain to reach the big explosion at the climax. These are sometimes called "idiot plots" because the characters need to be idiots to let various events move forward. They fail to notice something obvious (the broken window), or they forget to mention something important (the results of the autopsy), or they take shortcuts down dark alleys, even though they're aware that a mass murderer has just escaped from the insane asylum down the road. They're fools, and to paraphrase Mark Twain, they all deserve to be drowned together.

In the opposite and better kind of novel, however, characters control the plot. Properly motivated, their fears and desires set events in motion and cause the plot to proceed to a satisfying inevitable end. In his discussion of tragedy, Aristotle (might as well bring out the heavy hitters) emphasizes that an ideal plot is constructed so that, at the climax, reversal and recognition occur. "Reversal" means that events seemingly headed in one direction abruptly go in the opposite direction (good news turns out to be bad, or perhaps an assassin is assassinated). "Recognition" means that the main character achieves an important self-discovery, not always pleasant (in the case of Oedipus, he learns that he killed his father and married his mother). Sometimes the recognition causes the reversal. Other times the reversal causes the recognition. In either case, the character experiences a change (learns something, overcomes a flaw) that seems probable and inevitable, resulting in a satisfactory conclusion that ideally gives us something to think about. For a different view on these matters, read Robert McKee's *Story*. That theoretical book is primarily for screenwriters, but what he says is helpful to fiction writers as well.

At one time, it was fashionable to say that all plots could be reduced to five variations. This is how they were categorized: Man against man (forgive the sexist terminology). Man against nature. Man against himself. Man against society. Man against God. I stare at these categories, and I'm not sure what good they do me. They seem arbitrary and somewhat forced. The best I can say is that they emphasize the notion of conflict without which no plot can be interesting.

That's worth repeating. Without conflict, no plot can be interesting. Without conflict, you *don't have* a plot. Without conflict, all you're stuck with is high concept, a skinny, unfocused situation. "A madman tries to poison New York's water supply." So what? In life, that would be catastrophic, but in fiction, if all I do is read about a nutcase who tries to poison the city's water supply, frankly, I don't care.

The key word that needs elaboration is "tries." That word suggests an opposite force trying to stop him: a policeman, a federal agent, a psychiatrist, a water inspector, a plumber, anybody, as long as that person is the antagonist of the madman with the poison. Conflict. The question now is why does the madman want to poison the water, which means that chronology turns into causality—story evolves into plot. Why, why, why. Who is the man trying to stop the nutcase? How did this man learn about the threat to the water supply? Is the nutcase really as nutty as he first appears? Does the apparent madman perhaps have valid reasons (from his point of view) for the many deaths he wants to cause? As we ask more questions in our written conversation with ourselves, more details demand to be added until we create a coherent narrative with characters who do things for reasons we understand. Once we understand a person's motives, we sympathize with that person. Sympathy causes interest. Caring about these people, we want to know what happens next.

The more I look at those five categories of plots, the more I think five are too many. As far as I'm concerned, in the abstract there's only *one* plot, and it goes like this: A person or group or entity (an animal or an alien, whatever) *wants* something. Perhaps it's to survive a blizzard, to get married, to dominate the world, or to save a child trapped in a fire, whatever. Another person or group or entity (nature, for example, or a destructive inner self) throws up every barrier imaginable to stop that goal from being achieved.

A plot doesn't get any more basic. A quest and obstacles. That's narrative's unified field theory, the equivalent of $E=mc^2$. To turn that story into a plot, all you need to do is ask *why* each force wants what it does. In other words, add motive to conflict. The scope of the narrative can be large or small. What matters is the conviction with which the two forces compete with each other. In that sense, a man wanting to paint a house can be as compelling as a woman wanting to be the first astronaut to land on Mars, as long as you dramatize how important the goal is to the person straining to achieve it.

Another way to look at plot comes from the comparative study of mythology. In 1936, in his book *The Hero*, Lord Raglan identified the elements that many myths from various parts of the world share. He synthesized these into a twenty-two-stage pattern.

1. The hero's mother is a royal virgin.
2. His father is a king.
3. His father is often a near relative of his mother.
4. The circumstances of his conception are unusual.
5. He is reputed to be the son of a god.
6. At birth an attempt is made, usually by his father or his maternal grandmother, to kill him.
7. He is spirited away.
8. He is reared by foster parents in a far country.
9. We are told nothing of his childhood.

10. On reaching manhood he returns or goes to his future kingdom.

11. He has a victory over the king and/or a giant, dragon, or wild beast.

12. He marries a princess, often the daughter of his predecessor.

13. He becomes a king.

14. For a time he reigns uneventfully.

15. He prescribes laws.

16. Later he loses favor with the gods and/or his subjects.

17. He is driven from the throne and city.

18. He meets with a mysterious death.

19. He dies at the top of a hill.

20. His children, if any, do not succeed him.

21. His body is not buried.

22. He has one or more holy sepulchers.

Many heroes, ancient and modern, share several of these stages: Odysseus, Aeneas, King Arthur, Dante in *The Divine Comedy*, Alice in her *Wonderland*, Leopold Bloom in *Ulysses*, and Harry Potter, to name a few. The parallel with Jesus Christ comes to mind. Consider the pattern as a metaphor. The mother is a virgin, and the father is a king—many children view their parents in this fashion, hence the shock when they realize that their virgin mother actually has sex with their father king. The circumstances of conception are unusual—we're back to sex again; recall your puzzlement when you realized the strange act that your mother and father performed in order to create you. The child is a son of a god—for many children, the father *is* a god, not always benevolent. The father makes an attempt to kill the child—again the fearsome aspect of the father. The child is spirited away and reared by foster parents—some children fantasize that the families in which they live are not their true families, that they had special origins but now are forced to live in base conditions. As I write these words, I realize for the first time that all of this can apply to what I told you earlier about my troubled childhood. Perhaps you find metaphoric parallels with your youth, also.

The rest of the pattern works in a similar way. As adults, we have a victory over the king and/or a dragon (our parents). We marry and become royalty, reigning uneventfully for a time until our subjects (our children) become old enough to challenge our authority. We are driven from the throne (get old) and meet with a mysterious death (the greatest mystery of all). Our children do not succeed us—they can't; they're individuals, with lives of their own. We aren't buried—again this is metaphor inasmuch as we continue to exist in the memory of others and have many places (home, work, a favorite fishing spot) associated with us.

Other scholars looked deeper into this pattern: Otto Rank in *The Myth of the Birth of the Hero* and, particularly, Joseph Campbell in *The Hero with a Thousand Faces*. Indeed it was Campbell who reduced the pattern to three important basic stages: separation, initiation, and return. In the first act, childhood, we are dependent on others, our lives out of our control. Inevitably, something separates us from that childhood—we end our formal education, for example, or get married, or move away from home. In various ways, often with the aid of mentors (who are not always benign—harsh employers, for instance), we are initiated into adulthood, only to discover that the independence we craved is illusive. Finally, after a lifetime of hard-earned lessons, which lead through disillusionment to acceptance, we return to where we began (literally, we visit our parents and our hometowns, or in our imagination, we harken back to our childhoods) and discover how far we have come and how different the same things feel, and yet in a sense we haven't come far at all. Many of Dickens's novels come to mind here, especially *Great Expectations*, *David Copperfield*, and *Oliver Twist*.

This is a powerful pattern which Campbell associated with psychologist Carl Jung's theories of archetypes and the collective unconscious. According to Jung, there are certain basic universal structures in our minds that have analogies outside us and that we find inherently intriguing: our passage from birth through age to death represented metaphorically, say, by the passage of the sun and moon, the progress of the seasons, or, in terms of narrative, a hero's journey. Think of *The Odyssey*. Think of Steinbeck's *The Grapes of Wrath*. Campbell elaborated on these ideas in his *The Masks of God: Primitive Mythology*.

When George Lucas planned the first *Star Wars* series, he was heavily influenced by Campbell. When I wrote *First Blood*, I consciously used Campbell's separation-initiation-return pattern as my structure. In part one, Rambo (a mysterious young man in exile) comes to a strange town where he finds himself in conflict with the police chief (king and father figure). Eventually, Rambo is forced to break out of jail and escape into the mountains.

At that separation, part two begins, in which Rambo is initiated into metaphorical adulthood, surviving a series of tests and obstacles, proving himself superior to the king/father. The initiation concludes with Rambo's mystical experience in the bat cave (a rat cave in the film), his emotions so powerful that he transcends physical existence.

In part three, he returns to town (a metaphor for his youth and his boyhood home) but sees it all differently and finally destroys it along with the king/father. In turn, Rambo is killed by his mentor and alternate father figure (Colonel Trautman, the man who trained him in the military), who is also the mentor that Rambo's king/father came to rely on. That mentor's first name is Sam and is meant to be identified with *Uncle* Sam, the nickname for the system that created Rambo and then destroyed him. (In mythology, uncles are often ambiguous.)

The idea here is that certain plots have a universal psychological structure that gives them extra power. It would take a separate book for me to go into all the nuances of the theory and its application. Read Campbell. Read Christopher Vogler's *The Writer's Journey: Mythic Structure for Writers*. Do not apply the theory in a mechanical or literal fashion. Remember that you're dealing with metaphors. Once you internalize the theory, try to forget it. Only if it is second nature can you use it successfully.

I'll have more to say about plot when we get to lesson six, "The Tactics of Structure." For now, after that complicated discussion of one possible approach, it's useful to return to the basics. Plot equals conflict plus motivation. No matter how you proceed (perhaps you base your plot on institutions, as Arthur Hailey did in *Hotel* and *Airport*, or perhaps you base it on geographic location, as James Michener did in *Hawaii* and *Texas*), you can't go wrong if you constantly bear in mind the requirements of conflict and motivation. But before you think you've found the philosopher's stone and now have the power of transforming narrative lead into gold, consider this: The magic of a plot, the brilliance that distinguishes would-be writers from the real thing, is the ability to present conflict and motive in a fresh, ingenious way. Conflict and motive are (in John Barth's words) the obstacle race and the scavenger hunt that are metaphorically present (and sometimes literally) in every kind of novel. Seeking a fresh way to write about them, you face an obstacle race and a scavenger hunt of your own.

Character

P lot and character are intimately related. Flipping through an essential reference book, M. H. Abrams's *A Glossary of Literary Terms*, I'm reminded of a quote from Henry James: "What is character but the determination of incident? What is incident but the illustration of character?" The task is to get a satisfying proportion. As we saw in the previous lesson, sometimes plot controls character (in the worst case so arbitrarily that people in the story behave stupidly and unbelievably). By contrast, sometimes characters determine the plot, their needs and frustrations setting events in motion (in the worst case so leisurely and episodically that the story is, to paraphrase Ogden Nash, just one damned thing after another).

Film actor Steve McQueen once vented a fit of egotism by complaining that he couldn't understand why there were other characters in his movies. "Why can't they just make a movie about me, me, me?" While a few films and novels have tried to restrict themselves to one character (the classic example being Defoe's shipwrecked *Robinson Crusoe*, although even there Crusoe's companion Friday is eventually introduced), their meager numbers indicate how difficult it is to keep that kind of story interesting. We enjoy dialogue. We like characters interacting with one another. If you try a one-person drama (a single survivor of a plane crash, for example), you'll quickly realize how limiting it is to describe only that character's attempt to survive. You'll soon be tempted to introduce flashbacks involving the protagonist's relationship with other characters. You'll feel the urge to cut to scenes involving the rescuers.

Characters can be divided into various categories. Minor versus major is an obvious distinction. But as a drama teacher once told me, "there are no minor characters, only minor actors. If you're portraying a servant and your only job is to bring a cup of tea on stage and then leave, make sure you decide whether you like the person who ordered the tea and what your attitude should be when you set the cup down. Decide what your facial expression should be and how to move. Without upstaging the story, make the servant you're portraying a character and not merely an automaton."

The same advice applies to fiction. Consider this example:

> Joe got into the taxi.
> "Where to?" the driver asked.
> "Kennedy airport," Joe said.
> The driver pulled into traffic.

Nothing much happening here. Joe needs to get to Kennedy airport. He needs to use a taxi. The story evidently requires us to read about him going through the process. The taxi driver isn't even a minor character; he's a blank.

Now consider the following variation:

> Joe got into the taxi.
> "Where to?" the driver asked.
> "Kennedy airport," Joe said.
> The driver squinted, put on the thickest glasses that Joe had ever seen, and inched into traffic.

The business about the glasses happens quickly. It doesn't interfere with the progress of the story, but it adds a freshness that the scene previously didn't have. The idea of an almost sightless New York City taxi driver amuses me. If I wanted, I could imagine an entire story about him. But here I get what Hemingway called the tip of the iceberg. I sense the rest of the iceberg under the surface of the story. The incidental character gains a little something extra, and the effect required very few words.

When you're having your protagonist interact with clerks, maids, flight attendants, secretaries, and so on, look for opportunities to characterize those blanks. At the very least, give each an interesting physical detail.

> Joe went over to the clerk. "Let me see that necklace."
> The clerk put it on the counter.

The passage is bland. But what if we make a change?

> Joe went over to the clerk. "Let me see that necklace."
> The male clerk's slender fingers put the necklace on the counter.

Again, the addition happens swiftly. After all, we don't want to slow the story. But at the same time, we've added a slight depth. A male jewelry clerk with slender fingers. Is he self-conscious about those fingers? Or does he think they make him look sensitive? Perhaps he's foppish. Perhaps he's a safe cracker in training, slender delicate fingers being an asset to a safe cracker. We'll never know. The story has already progressed. But we sense a little lower layer. Make it a habit to respect your walk-on characters and find efficient ways to make them seem fuller. To paraphrase that drama teacher, there are no minor characters, only minor authors.

As for major characters, it's useful to borrow E. M. Forster's logic and think of them either as types or as multidimensional. Forster defines a type as someone who is constructed around a single quality and can be defined in a sentence or two. Forster isn't being pejorative when he calls a character a type (his alternative word is "flat"). On the contrary, he feels that types have many virtues. Necessary to move most stories along, they are easily recognized when they appear, and easily remembered. In his opinion, all of Dickens's major characters are types, but that statement doesn't prevent Forster from thinking that Dickens is one of the best English novelists.

Easily summarized. A single quality or two. On that basis, the main characters of most popular fiction are types. Their authors might do their best to give them interesting backgrounds and winning personalities and to pile on details about where they were born and whether their parents loved them. In essence, though, that detective or judge or pilot or gangster or unhappy wife or cheating husband or dying grandmother will only be a more or less fleshed-out version of a detective, judge, pilot, gangster, etc. They are defined by their plot functions in the story. In Mario Puzo's *The Godfather*, Don Corleone is an impoverished Sicilian who comes to the United States and pursues the American Dream by becoming a mobster. Sonny is the hot-headed son. Michael is the son who wants a legitimate profession but gets drawn into the family business and turns out to be brilliant at it. Puzo's achievement is that he gave these characters enough fascinating attributes to make the reader forget that they are types.

What makes a character multidimensional? According to Forster, it's someone who is difficult to describe succinctly. Someone who is capable of surprising us. Someone whose complexity becomes more manifest each time we read about that person. Looked at in this way, few characters can be considered multidimensional. Forster includes Madame Bovary, all the major characters in *War and Peace*, as well as those in Dostoyevsky and some in Proust. Not many. Note that these are characters who control their stories, who give the impression of acting on their own and not being under the command of their authors. They are not defined by their plot functions but rather by who they are, and that takes us back to the dichotomy between plot-oriented stories and character-oriented stories. Compare Paul Gallico's *The Poseidon Adventure* with Kafka's "The Metamorphosis." In the first, a tidal wave hits a passenger ship and knocks it upside down. In the second, a man wakes up one morning and discovers that he has become a cockroach. In the first, the passengers struggle through an overturned universe to reach the ocean's surface. We don't much care who they are. A selection of representative types is all that's needed. The struggle is what's important, and if the author gets too deeply into describing the characters, we skim the pages until we get to the next incident. In the second narrative, however, the entire point of the story is the character of the man who becomes the cockroach. Who *is* he, and how is he going to react to his new condition? The more dimensions he has, the better.

Which is harder to write, types or multidimensional characters? I suggest types are harder because the narratives in which they appear impose limitations that make it more difficult to be creative. In my travels, I once visited the home of a respected mainstream novelist who was also the director of a well-known writers' school. He took me to his study and asked me to read the first fifty pages of a novel he was writing. The project was an experiment for him, he explained. A gangster story set in the Caribbean. His tone made it clear that he had decided to show genre writers how easy it was to write a commercial story and how an author with a serious literary background would be much better at it.

While he watched, I read his pages with increasing discomfort. It's not that they were awful. To the contrary, each page was beautifully written. But they didn't hold together. Dependent entirely on character, the narrative wandered. There were sudden long digressions that explained the main character's background. Equally digressive sections of italics interrupted the story to elaborate the fantasies of the main character. It was almost impossible to follow the narrative. The digressive techniques were the same as those that he used in his "serious" novels, which were brilliant multidimensional character studies but which also rambled and required no rules. Those techniques had no place in a gangster novel, which required that the characters serve the plot. Eventually the novelist understood the difference and admitted that he wasn't interested in subordinating his techniques and characters to rules that certain kinds of narrative impose. His gangster novel was never published.

I'm not suggesting that one approach is better than the other. What I *am* suggesting is that narratives with rules are more difficult to write, especially when it comes to deciding how much or how little to develop your characters. In plot-driven stories, the goal is to create the illusion that the characters are more than types. That's hard to do without impeding the flow of the narrative.

When inventing a character, it's helpful to remember Hemingway's iceberg theory. What's on the surface should imply an unstated depth. How do you achieve this? Borrow a device that many stage dramatists employ. In your written conversation with yourself, create a detailed history for your character. Where and when was the character born? What were the occupations and personalities of the parents? Were there brothers and sisters? What was the character's attitude toward them? What about playmates? Did the character enjoy being young? Where did the character go to school? Keep asking and answering similar questions until you reach the point where the character enters the story. Most of this background will never appear in print. What you're trying to get is a sense of this person so that you know the way the character thinks, talks, and dresses, etc. If a background detail seems relevant, it's easily inserted in dialogue or a moment of reflection. As for the details that are left out, Hemingway explained that the reader will have a sense of them as strongly as if they were included, provided that the details that *are* included have weight.

The key to your character is what he or she wants and what obstacles must be overcome to achieve that goal (the motive and conflict without which there cannot be a plot). But once you've prepared your character sketch, once you've decided to set a character into motion on the page, you need to come to terms with how to present that person: the difference between telling and showing (what Forster calls describing from the outside or else from within). This is a question of viewpoint, about which I'll have much to say a few lessons from now. At the moment, it's enough to understand that telling tends to be vague and showing tends to be vivid.

Here are two examples of telling:

Alexey Fyodorovich Karamazov was the third son of Fyodor Pavlovich Karamazov, a landowner of our district, who became notorious in his own day (and is still remembered among us) because of his tragic and mysterious death, which occurred exactly thirteen years ago and which I shall relate in its proper place. For the present all I shall say about this "landowner" (as we used to call him, though he hardly ever lived on his estate) is that he was a strange sort of individual...

—Fyodor Dostoyevsky, *The Brothers Karamazov,* translation by David Magarshack

Eleanor Vance was thirty-two years old when she came to Hill House. The only person in the world she genuinely hated, now that her mother was dead, was her sister. She disliked her brother-in-law and her five-year-old niece, and she had no friends. This was owing largely to the eleven years she had spent caring for her invalid mother, which had left her with some proficiency as a nurse and an inability to face strong sunlight without blinking. She could not remember ever being truly happy in her adult life.

—Shirley Jackson, *The Haunting of Hill House*

In these examples, the character is at a distance. We're aware that we're being told about someone. The example from Shirley Jackson is almost the character sketch that I suggested you write in your conversation with yourself. In the extreme, the lack of immediacy in this technique can draw attention to itself.

Now here are two examples of showing:

Radclif eyed the boy over the rim of his beer glass, not caring much for the looks of him. He had his notions of what a "real" boy should look like, and this kid somehow offended him. He was too pretty, too delicate and fair-skinned; each of his features was shaped with a sensitive accuracy, and a girlish tenderness softened his eyes, which were brown and very large.

—Truman Capote, *Other Voices, Other Rooms*

Mr. George Smiley was not naturally equipped for hurrying in the rain, least of all at dead of night . . . Small, podgy, and at best middle-aged, he was by appearance one of London's meek who do not inherit the earth. His legs were short, his gait everything but agile, his dress costly, ill-fitting, and extremely wet. His overcoat, which had a hint of widowhood about it, was of that black loose weave which is designed to retain moisture. Either the sleeves were too long or his arms were too short, for . . . when he wore his mackintosh, the cuffs all but concealed the fingers.

—John le Carre, *Tinker, Tailor, Soldier, Spy*

In these two examples, the narrator is more or less invisible. The characters are presented directly, in a concrete fashion. Each is shown to us in specific terms.

Because the second set of examples is vivid, it's tempting to think that showing is the better method. Unfortunately, showing is also more difficult. It requires painstaking plotting in order to establish scenes in which general information about a character is dramatized in specific terms. Go back and look at the Jackson quote. In a paragraph, she provides information that it would take considerable pages to establish if Jackson felt obliged only to show us the character rather than also tell us about her. In practice, a certain amount of telling is inevitable. Otherwise, a story might never be completed. But it's useful to know which method you're using and to steer from telling to showing as soon as possible in order to provide the immediacy that is more likely to capture a reader's attention. As we'll see in the lesson about third-person viewpoint, this is usually a contrast between the omniscient viewpoint and the third-person limited. You can shift from telling to showing (from omniscient to limited), but once you're showing, once you're in a third-person limited, you will jar the reader if you go back to an omniscient narrator telling about a character in general terms.

We're not finished with characterization. It's so crucial to storytelling that the topic will inevitably come up when we discuss many other aspects of fiction writing: description and dialogue, for example. But at the moment, let's conclude this theoretical discussion with another of Forster's observations. For him, one of the central appeals of fiction is that

> In daily life, we never understand each other, neither complete clairvoyance nor complete confessional exists. We know each other approximately, by external signs, and these serve well enough as a basis for society and even for intimacy. But people in a novel can be understood completely by the reader, if the novelist wishes; their inner as well as their outer life can be exposed.

I enjoy this paradox: We call a fully drawn character "lifelike" when in fact we can never know someone in life as well as we have known that character in fiction. To the degree that we are privy to a character's thoughts and emotions, the experience is totally *un*realistic, however magical. "That is why novels . . . can solace us," Forster says. "They suggest a more comprehensible and thus a more manageable human race."

The Importance of Research

Write what you know about—that's a common rule in creative writing classes. It sounds like good advice, but what does it mean? In the first half of the twentieth century, American writers were often expected to travel, gain a wealth of experience, and use that as the basis for their fiction. Jack London wrote about his adventures in the Klondike gold rush. Hemingway volunteered as a Red Cross ambulance driver in World War I. Steinbeck accompanied the Depression-ravaged "Okies" as they left their dust-bowl homes and struggled across the country toward California and what they hoped would be the Promised Land. Norman Mailer went to World War II. Jack Kerouac went on the road. John Dos Passos. Nelsen Algren. A list of this kind of reportorial author would be extensive.

Not that they were all manly men doing manly things. One of my favorites, Edith Wharton, is another good example. A member of the old-money New York Jones family, she shocked her strict society by divorcing her emotionally unstable, embezzling husband and establishing permanent residence in France. Earlier, she shocked old New York even more severely by committing the ultimate horror of seeming to work for a living (she didn't need the money) as a writer, an activity she always dreamed about. Often in her fiction (the best of which, for me, is *The Age of Innocence*), she provided a rare eyewitness account of what it was like to be part of Manhattan's repressive, secretive high society in the last third of the 1800s. As with the other writers I mentioned, a major appeal of Wharton's subject is its authenticity of detail, its report from the trenches: the novelist as social historian describing the calling cards left at elegant brownstone mansions, the fashion-able carriages parading along Fifth Avenue, and the female archery contests (one of the few physical exercises permitted to proper women).

This live-it-then-write-it tradition changed after the Second World War when returning soldiers took advantage of the G.I. Bill to get a free college education. Because many of them wanted to write about their war experiences, courses for fiction writers gained a popularity they hadn't enjoyed before. Writers' programs multiplied. But after the veterans graduated, students who hadn't been in the war took their place, and these apprentice writers gained the experience of literature rather than the tastes and touches of events in the world. By the 1960s, a major trend in academically approved American fiction was to use literature as its subject. Writers wrote about writing. Technique became theme. Many excellent books came out of this approach, John Barth's collection, *Lost in the Funhouse,* for instance, in which a narrator habitually pauses a story to comment on the way the story is being written. But the effect was to narrow the subject matter of appren-tice writers. At present, the only major social-historian American novelist who comes to mind is Tom Wolfe. Otherwise, critically praised fiction tends to be of two types: self-referential, very aware that it is fiction, constantly drawing attention to that fact, and frequently referring to fiction by other writers; or else inward oriented, focusing on the interior, emotional details of a main character who is often a version of the author.

Write what you know about. That's what these writers are doing. With exceptions, their formative years were spent in college. They write what they know about, which is to say books and themselves. Apart from continuing to read and to go about their lives, they don't need to do any research. *They* are their subject matter. But there are other approaches, and I think it would be beneficial for fiction-writing teachers to tell their students, "Get out of here. Travel. Join the Peace Corps. Fight forest fires. Experience as much as you can. Write about it. If you have trouble with technique, come back a couple of years from now, and we'll talk. Class dismissed."

I like this advice because one of the occupational hazards of being writers is that all the time we're sitting at our desks, laboring over stories, life passes us by. To keep things fresh, I long ago decided that between projects I ought to find stimulating new things to do, activities that would be fascinating to learn and (not incidentally) useful in a book. On a simple level, that means taking advantage of vacations to research locales, seeking out a new, interesting place each time. I've been to the Mexican resort of Cancun and to the Mayan ruins nearby, for example. Loved the experience, used it in a novel (*Assumed Identity*), been there, done it, won't go back again no matter how good a time I had. There's too much else to do and learn. If a vacation offers no more than the traditional lying on the beach, reading, and drinking rum and Coke, I won't have anything to do with it. For me, a vacation isn't appealing unless it involves unfamiliar activities that are potentially useable in a book.

On another level, research means immersing yourself in your subject matter. Back in the early 1970s, I began making notes for my second novel, *Testament*, realizing that many scenes would depict wilderness survival. The trouble was, everything I knew about the subject came from movies. A library addict, I decided that I'd better read some books about staying alive in the wilderness, but after going through several, I got the unsettling feeling that the writers of those books were basing their information on other books. They weren't giving me a vivid sense of what it was like to be in the dangerous situations I wanted to depict. Gradually it became obvious that I needed hands-on experience. After I read a magazine article about the National Outdoor Leadership School, an organization dedicated to teaching people how to experience the wilderness safely and responsibly, I sent for its catalogue, chose the course that best suited my requirements, and arranged my schedule so I could attend.

In those days, I was still teaching at the University of Iowa. As soon as the spring semester ended, I drove to Lander, Wyoming, where NOLS is based, and for the next thirty-five days, along with twenty-nine other students, I carried a sixty-pound backpack through the Wind River mountains. We learned about camping without a trace, crossing wild streams, living off the land, navigating with a compass and a contour map, rock climbing, rappelling, surviving blizzards (it was June, but we had seven days of fierce snow), digging snow caves, avoiding hypothermia, dealing with altitude sickness, and so on. For our graduation exercise, our instructors showed us a spot on a map and told us that in three days trucks would be there to pick us up. The site was fifty miles away (easy) but on the other side of the Continental Divide (gulp), and oh, by the way, we weren't allowed to eat anything for the entire three days. The idea was to replicate an emergency situation, to give us the confidence that even without food we could survive for the three days of hard climbing and hiking it would take us to get to the pickup spot. Sounds daunting, but all of us managed it. I lost twenty-five pounds during the course and came back with invaluable firsthand knowledge that made the survival scenes in *Testament* seem authentic. All these years later, my NOLS training still shows up in my novels.

It's worth emphasizing that the experience wasn't good only for my fiction—it was good for *me*. Instead of being limited by writing only about what I already knew, I decided to write books about subjects that I wanted to learn, using the opportunity for research to make my life fuller. I developed a pattern—do the reading, conduct interviews, then get hands-on experience. James Thurber once wrote a story about a character named Walter Mitty, an ordinary man with adventure-filled fantasies. Every writer can be like Mitty, with the advantage that in dramatizing the products of our imaginations we're able, via our research, to live our fantasies.

For my novels, I've gone to the Bill Scott Raceway in West Virginia, where the U.S. government's Diplomatic Security Service sends its agents to learn antiterrorist driving maneuvers. While I was there, the Canadian version of Delta Force was also getting driving instruction. I learned how to do forward and backward 180 degree spins at forty-five miles an hour. I learned to do this both in the driver's seat and in the passenger's seat. In the latter case, my instructor slumped over the steering wheel as if shot. I had to use my left foot and hand to control the vehicle at high speed while doing the spins or whatever else was necessary (ramming a barricade, for example) to foil an attack.

In 1986, I attended the G. Gordon Liddy Academy. I specify the year because that was the only time the academy was offered, once each in Florida, New York, and California. The course (day and night including weekends) lasted three weeks and was intended for security and law enforcement specialists. After checking my background to make sure I wouldn't abuse the potentially dangerous information I'd be given, the academy allowed me to participate. The instructors were ex–CIA, ex–FBI, ex–DEA, and numerous other ex-operatives of various high-level alphabet-soup government agencies. A medical examiner from Dade County taught us about crime-scene investigation and how to use the fumes of Miracle Glue to get fingerprints off a corpse. A polygraph expert taught us the principles of a lie-detector test and theoretical ways to foil it. An ex-member of Israeli intelligence taught us about airport security. A home-invasion specialist taught us about locks and intrusion detectors. From an ex-member of military intelligence, I learned about undercover work, the subject of *Assumed Identity*. From an ex–U.S. marshal who was part of the team responsible for guarding John Hinckley Jr. after he shot President Reagan, I learned about executive protection (sophisticated bodyguarding) and used it as the subject of *The Fifth Profession*. I learned about bombs, electronic surveillance, and hostage negotiation.

But the research doesn't need to be sensational—I've also enjoyed learning about photography and using eggs to make tempera paint. Whatever turns you on. If you have an obviously dramatic profession, such as paramedic or deep-sea explorer, by all means write about what you know. That's what forensic anthropologist Kathy Reichs did in *Death du Jour*. So did Patricia Cornwell, who once had a clerical job in a medical examiner's office. For most of us, though, life is ordinary. Writing about what I already know isn't half as stimulating as learning something that interests me and then inventing a plot that allows me to write about it.

The point is, research should be considered a reward and not a penance that you need to go through before you start writing. If you don't have a strong motivation to learn about the background of your story, maybe you'd better reconsider how interesting that story is. At the least, research gives you the chance to avoid looking foolish. Too often, authors are lulled into thinking that the details of this or that subject depicted in movies bear a resemblance to actuality. How often in movies have you seen a detective find a plastic bag of white powder, slice it open, stick his finger in the powder, taste it, and wisely announce that the powder is heroin? The scene looks dramatic, but the truth is, no detective in his right mind would taste that powder. It might be bleach. It might be rat poison. A moment's reflection tells us how phony the scene is. Real detectives laugh at it. Yet I frequently read that scene in books, just as I come across scenes in which a character shoots a gas tank, causing a car to explode. Unless you use incendiary bullets, that's impossible. You could shoot ordinary bullets at a gas tank all day and not cause it to blow up (I've done it). But it happens in movies all the time. Novelists can be so conditioned by what they see on the screen that they don't do their research. As a consequence, some of their scenes can be as flawed as the ones I just described.

If you're writing about an emergency ward, don't rely on television programs to give you details, which can be so wrong they're often ridiculed by real physicians. Go to a hospital. Get your details firsthand. The same goes for courtrooms, police stations, morgues, newsrooms, whatever. An on-site look will give you unexpected dramatic details that make your scene feel authentic and prompt your readers to think, *Gosh, I didn't know that*, one of the highest compliments a writer can receive. Make it a habit to be an investigative reporter as much as a fiction writer. Take notes. Keep a small camera handy, the kind that fits in a pocket and doesn't draw attention to you. If an opportunity comes along and you don't have a camera with you, buy a disposable one from a photo shop or a drug store. In case you can't visit a place, find books or magazines that have photos of it. Talk to people who have been there. Read as many non-fiction books on the subject as you can. Use the Internet. In one of my books, *Burnt Sienna*, the airport in Nice, France, is a major setting. To learn about it, I conducted an Internet search for "Nice, France, airport." Presto: I suddenly had five dense pages of information, including a description of the airport's two terminals. Make sure, however, that your Internet source is reliable. So-called chat rooms are notorious for providing inaccurate information. Take no background in your plot for granted. If a character gets on a plane, do your best to make sure that the time and destination of that flight are as you claim they are. Find factual mistakes before the mistakes have so controlled your scenes that they can't be corrected without destroying the sequence of events.

Stephen Crane was a model researcher. The sheltered son of a Methodist minister, Crane knew that he had to learn about life if he was going to write about it. He became a newspaper reporter, roamed New York's slums, and adapted gritty details that he'd seen and felt into his fiction, notably in *Maggie: A Girl of the Streets* and in "The Open Boat," a story based on his 1897 near death after he was shipwrecked off the coast of Florida on his way to report on the Cuban insurrection. But Crane's triumph of research was *The Red Badge of Courage*, a Civil War novel that feels so authentic many readers and reviewers assumed that he was a veteran of the Civil War. However, Crane published that novel in 1895 when he was 24. He couldn't possibly have been in the Civil War, which ended in 1865. To make his novel seem true, he interviewed veterans of the Civil War, read accounts of battles, particularly the one at Chancellorsville, and studied Matthew Brady's photographs of the war.

Hemingway did much the same when writing *A Farewell to Arms*. That 1929 novel about the First World War is widely assumed to be autobiographical. But when we compare the novelist's life with the events in the novel, it's clear that Hemingway wasn't in Italy during the time in the book. Moreover, he wasn't in the same area of the war. The novel's great middle section, the historical retreat from Caporetto, has an "I was there" vividness, but it all came out of Hemingway's research. Using his newspaper reporter's skills, he interviewed veterans of that retreat. He read old newspaper articles. He studied histories. Renowned for making readers feel the accuracy of what he described, Hemingway actually relied on maps and on travel books such as Baedeker's for details about many of the places that he didn't visit. For more on Hemingway's research techniques, read Michael Reynolds's *Hemingway's First War: The Making of "A Farewell to Arms."*

But research also involves learning about the kind of fiction you write. One of the greatest disappointments for a writer is to work on something that's intended to be unique only to discover that it's been done countless times before. When I taught at the University of Iowa, a student came to my office and told me he'd decided to write a detective novel. I applauded his enthusiasm and said that I looked forward to the result. Six months later, he returned with a thick manuscript. Over the next few days, I read the novel with increasing unease. What he had done, with no sense of irony, was to re-create a 1940s private-eye story. It was well written and absolutely unpublishable, I told him.

"But you said it's well written."

"Correct. In 1940, publishers would have jumped at it. But now it's old-fashioned. No matter how well written, it isn't going to attract a publisher if there are hundreds of books just like it. Good writing isn't enough. You need a vision, a new approach. How much research did you do?"

"Research?"

"Yes, how many private-eye novels did you read? What about *Black Mask* magazine? Did you find any good histories of the genre?"

"*Black Mask*? Histories?"

It turned out that the student hadn't read anything at all, whether fiction or fact, about private eyes. He was a fan of Humphrey Bogart detective movies. Basically, he had imagined an alternative version of the movies *The Maltese Falcon* and *The Big Sleep* without opening a book by Dashiell Hammett or Raymond Chandler. I explained that private-eye fiction had gone in all sorts of directions since the 1940s and that if he was serious about writing a book in that genre, he needed to read all its masters.

"And it wouldn't hurt to read some nonfiction books about what real private detectives do," I added. "Look in the Yellow Pages. Make an appointment to talk to a real investigator. Try to find out what it's like to *be* an investigator. Give us a book that has details we've never come across before. Read Joe Gores. He's a real private eye who writes novels about what it's like to be a real private eye."

The student's jaw hung open as he lost his innocence.

"What's the value of imitating a movie or another writer?" I asked him. "Make other writers imitate *you*."

That discussion could apply to every type of fiction. Whether it's postmodernism, social satire, political analysis, science fiction, a romance, or a Western, you need to be an expert in it. You need to know its history so well that you can teach it. You need to have assimilated its tradition so completely that your fiction adds to that tradition instead of being redundant.

In a broader sense, you need to be familiar with the classics. That might seem obvious, but most of the apprentice novelists I meet at various writing conferences haven't read F. Scott Fitzgerald, let alone Emily Bronte. Imagine a beginning writer who one day gets an idea to write a novel that is told entirely by various connected first-person narratives. What an original concept! that writer thinks. Bursting with enthusiasm, he or she spends months composing it and at last asks an experienced reader to give a judgment.

"Well, it's nicely done as far as it goes," the reader concludes. "The trouble is, it doesn't go far enough. *Wuthering Heights* is the model for this technique, and you haven't done anything new with it."

"What's *Wuthering Heights*?"

Next to an utter lack of ability, the worst flaw I can think of for a would-be writer is ignorance about literary history. It's absurd to imagine a brain surgeon who doesn't know the history and principles of brain surgery, yet many aspiring writers assume that because words fall out of their mouths every day, they need no other qualification to write fiction. Obviously, not everyone has the time and money to get a college degree in literature. But lists of important literary works are readily available. Read David Denby's *Great Books*, for example. Go to your local library and get help from a reference person. Contact the English department at your local college, get the office phone numbers for some of its professors, then ask those professors to send you a list of the books they teach in their courses. You'll be surprised how many are glad to help. Be organized. Pick an area: the nineteenth-century American novel, for example. Read the books in chronological order. If something puzzles you, ask the librarian or the professor to recommend an analytical book that'll clear up the puzzle. Some of the novels will be a joy, others a headache. The process won't always be easy. It certainly won't be quick. But literary innocence isn't a virtue for a writer. You need to know that what you're writing isn't derivative and stale.

The student who brought me that well-written but unpublishable imitation of a 1940s private-eye novel? His name is Jon Jackson, and he eventually wrote a series of respected police novels set in Detroit and featuring a version of a real-life roving instant-response police squad (*Hit on the House*). It turns out that Jon had a brother in the Detroit police department. He went to his brother, did his research, and wrote something that had never been done before. Instead of being an imitator, Jon's now part of the history of the genre. The next up-and-coming detective writer needs to take *Jon's* work into account. That should be *your* objective as well. No matter the type of fiction you write, you should want to be an innovator, and research is crucial to achieving that goal.

The Tactics of Structure

Beginning writers sometimes tell me, "Working on short stories is so hard I can't imagine how I'll ever find the time and energy to complete a novel." I know exactly what they mean. The shortest time I've taken to write a novel is nine months, and that was working on it every day. More often, I needed between one and two years. On a couple of occasions, *three* years. Working just about every day. But if you're a beginning writer, you don't have that luxury. By definition, you're not supporting yourself as a writer. You have a job; you're in school; you're raising a family. To write, you need to stay up late, get up extra early, and squeeze hours from your weekends. A short story is daunting but manageable. Contemplating a novel, however, is like studying the horizon—it recedes infinitely.

To accomplish the task, the goal has to be redefined. When I sit down to write a novel, I don't think of it as a novel. Oh, sure, I've made my preparations. I know the scope of the plot and the nature of the characters. But if I keep reminding myself of the size of the job, if I constantly bear in mind that I'll be sitting at this same spot a year from now, working on the same project, I'll quit with exhaustion before I get started. For me, the goal isn't to write a novel. It's to write five pages a day. They're not perfect. They need frequent revision down the road. But at least they exist.

If you're someone who doesn't have the luxury of writing all day, restrict your goal to so many words per day or week. The mathematics is interesting. A page a day is 365 pages a year, the length of a novel. The key is to subdivide the huge task of a novel into smaller steps. By achieving the manageable goal you've set for yourself, you'll have a sense of daily accomplishment. Focus your attention on the short term, and the novel will take care of itself.

When thinking this way, it helps to be aware of your novel's structure. One way is to divide it into three acts. I've done several books (*First Blood* and *Testament* among them) that were so consciously structured in this manner that I used Part One, Part Two, and Part Three as the names of the divisions in the book. Reaching the end of a part was reason to be proud—something measurable had been accomplished. Within each part, there were separate smaller sections. Reaching the end of each of those sections was another cause for celebration.

Another way to divide a book is by visualizing the traditional narrative elements of beginning, middle, climax, and conclusion. It's useful to imagine this pattern in terms of a modified triangle, something John Barth notes in "Lost in the Funhouse," an essay about writing as much as it's a ground-breaking short story.

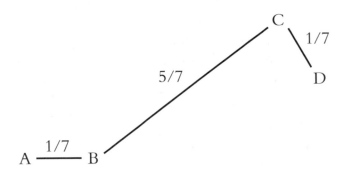

Interrupting his narrative to comment on the techniques he's using, Barth notes, "AB represents the exposition, B the introduction of conflict, BC the 'rising action,' complication, or development of the conflict, C the climax, or turn of the action, CD the denouement, or resolution of the conflict." Most narratives have a structure that can be represented in this fashion. Something about the logic of stories demands this approach. We can violate the convention, but we'd better have (as Barth does in his story) an awfully valid reason for doing so.

The proportion of the triangle is instructive. AB, the setup, is about as long as CD, the aftermath. BC, the complication, takes the most room. If we divide the triangle into sevenths, AB is one-seventh, BC five-sevenths, and CD one-seventh. I'm not proposing that as an ideal proportion. Some plots divide better into fifths. Henry James did *The Ambassadors* in twelve numbered parts that are really two groups of sixes.

1 2 3 4 <u>5</u> 6

7 8 9 10 <u>11</u> 12

The last six parts mirror the first six parts. Each group can be graphed as a triangle, with 5 and 11 as the climax of each.

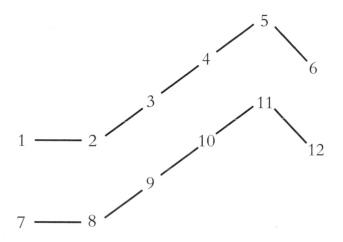

Whatever the proportion, the elements of the story need to feel in balance with one another, AB and CD not too long or short in relation to BC. Don't get preoccupied with the details of the geometry. Most true storytellers construct the triangle intuitively. If there's a problem of proportion, you can fix it in your final draft. For now, it's helpful to know where you are in the triangle. If you finished the introductory section of your plot, recognize your accomplishment and pat yourself on the back. Subdividing a novel to make it feel less imposing, you moved forward.

Chapters, too, can be considered in terms of the triangle. With each new scene, you need to establish time, place, and new characters while reintroducing characters who already appeared: AB. Then you need to dramatize the action of the scene, its purpose for being in the book: BC. Finally you need to get out of the scene and into the next one: CD. Nineteenth-century novels tended to have long chapters that felt like novels in miniature. With each new chapter, the reader had the sense that fresh machinery was being brought into place, that exposition was starting anew. Recent novels, influenced by the rapid pace of movies, tend to have shorter chapters, with greater speed from one to the other, avoiding exposition at the start of a scene, going straight to the purpose for the scene, then getting out of the scene and into the next without any denouement.

Novelist/screenwriter William Goldman talks about this technique in *Adventures in the Screen Trade*, suggesting that the key to constructing a sequence of scenes is to omit their beginnings and ends and jump from middle to middle. In other words, AB and CD are implied while only BC is dramatized. The triangle is still present, but parts of it are invisible. In nineteenth-century structure (using modern tone), a chapter might begin as follows:

> The next morning, Robert hurriedly dressed, ignored breakfast, and rushed outside, covering two blocks before he managed to find an empty taxi. Sweating from his exertion, he sat rigidly on the taxi's torn back seat, stiff with impatience as the driver got stuck in one traffic tangle after another. An excruciating thirty minutes later, the taxi stopped at its brownstone destination. Robert thrust some money at the driver and bolted out. Ignoring a sudden rain that drenched him, he charged up the building's steps two at a time, burst into his lawyer's office, and demanded that the secretary show him in at once.

Not immortal prose, but in my defense I didn't have much to work with. I've cheated by using intense verbs and adjectives, but the fact is, nothing much is happening. Robert got up, got dressed, hired a taxi, sat for a half hour, reached his lawyer's office, and demanded to be allowed in. A movie would get rid of all this and start the scene directly in the lawyer's office. In a novel, that direct method might not be a bad idea, either. Suppose the chapter starts *this* way: "Robert shoved the door open so hard that it banged against the wall. His lawyer, a lean man with a dark mustache, jerked his head up in surprise." The ensuing confrontation will imply everything that was in the discarded paragraph. The scene gets directly to the point, and once that point is made, we don't need a denouement in which Robert leaves the office and hires another taxi. Skip to a strong part of the next scene. Unless you're writing a novel whose manner is intentionally that of a nineteenth-century novel, your work will often benefit by cutting the beginning and end of the triangle in each scene. Start with dialogue. Start with activity. Conclude with something strong. But don't start and finish with a summary of the boring things your main character did between dramatic scenes. Whenever I sense that the pace of a sequence of chapters is dragging, I try an experiment and cut the first and last paragraph of each chapter. Usually I've fallen into the trap of including an unnecessary AB and CD.

The novel-writing experience that taught me the most about structure was *The Brotherhood of the Rose*. My previous five novels were roughly three-hundred manuscript pages long. But the popularity of three-inch-thick books by authors such as James Michener led publishers to consider a three-hundred-page manuscript as slight. Then, too, the new-at-the-time chain stores Waldenbooks and B. Dalton gained importance in the market-place. Large stacks of books displayed prominently became a factor in promoting titles. Because hardbacks generally come in two sizes, five-by-seven and six-by-nine, the latter was obviously more suited for large displays. Adjusting to the market, my agent suggested that I lengthen my manuscripts to six hundred pages so they could be in the more conspicuous format. Hardly the greatest reason to write a long book, but the more I thought about it, the more it seemed an interesting technical challenge.

Even so, it wasn't going to be easy, I realized. In my previous novel, *Blood Oath*, I had attempted a longer book (five hundred and fifty manuscript pages), only to have my editor suggest so many trims that the final draft was three hundred pages. (The editor's cuts were justified, by the way.) In my first attempt to write a longer book, I had mistakenly expanded my scenes and descriptions but had not done the same with the plot. Basically, the editor had merely cut overdone set decoration. I came away with the understanding that a bigger book meant more incident, not more description.

Henry James compared the structure of novels to the architecture of buildings. When moving from *Blood Oath* to *The Brotherhood of the Rose*, I kept that metaphor in mind. Faced with the aesthetic challenge of composing a book whose length would be twice as long as any I'd done before, I felt a little like an architect trying to design a huge building, wondering how on Earth I would keep the entire enterprise from collapsing. What finally carried me through was the advice I gave earlier. Subdivide. If the separate parts are solid, the whole will stand. Thus I came to think of a long book as a collection of building blocks that are disguised novellas. Each pseudonovella dramatizes an important arc of the story, but with AB and CD in each of them minimized, they flow from one to the other without the jerking stop and start that a sequence of true novellas would cause.

In thinking this way, I was influenced by another fiction writer/literary theorist: Edgar Allan Poe. He wrote several essays about writing, but the two most influential are "The Philosophy of Composition" and "The Poetic Principle," which explain his notions about unity of effect and the single sitting. Basically, Poe was worried about the attention span of his readers. In reading an epic like *Paradise Lost*, our attention inevitably wearies after a time, he said. No matter how brilliantly Milton created particular passages, we can't possibly appreciate all of them. As we tire, we fail to catch the genius in the lines. The epic begins to seem dull in spots. Finally we quit reading at a haphazard spot. When we come back, our attention is challenged as we try to reenter the story in the middle of a passage. Gradually, we become in tune with the words. Passages again seem brilliant until our attention wearies again and the book once more seems dull. Interestingly, if we reread the book but start on page 20, the rhythm of our attention will be different. Alert, we find formerly dull-seeming passages to be lively. Weary, we wonder why we thought that what now seems a dull passage ever had any life. Troubled by these observations, Poe wondered how he could write something that wouldn't suffer from the necessarily limited attention of his readers. His recommendation was to stay away from long works. In prose, he said, the short story was the ideal form because its length could be calculated on the basis of the reader's attention span. Only in works designed to be read in a single sitting could a writer expect the reader to appreciate the unity and artistry of the composition, Poe concluded.

How long is a single sitting, though? An hour? Forty minutes? In our age of channel surfing and MTV's frantic pacing, many people can't sit still. Even determined readers have trouble finding sustained blocks of time in which to enjoy a book. Our phones ring. Our bladders insist. Every writer knows the frustration of having persuaded a friend or a spouse to read a new story only to have the reading interrupted by a dog who knocks something over or a neighbor who drops in. The reader usually can't understand why the writer is frustrated. "Don't worry," the reader says. "I'll finish it later." But the writer knows that the story's carefully created subtleties won't be fully appreciated— because what was meant to be read in one sitting will now take more. With the story's structure accidentally fractured, it's hard for the reader to remember plot elements encountered in the previous sitting, let along recall nuances and link them to the continuation of the story.

Keeping all this in mind, I tried to accommodate my long novel to the reader's attention span by structuring *The Brotherhood of the Rose* so that each part could be read in a single sitting, roughly an hour, which seemed to me about fifty manuscript pages. To compartmentalize each unit, I gave it a title, hoping that when the reader finished a section and came to the title for the next, the obvious break would be a signal to stop if fatigue set in. The last thing I wanted was for the reader to start a new section but stop after a few pages, in which case the section's unity of effect would be destroyed.

Thus my table of contents looked like this. Out of context, the titles won't mean anything, but note the symmetry.

PROLOGUE: THE ABELARD SANCTION
  Refuge
  Safe Houses/Rest Homes
BOOK ONE: SANCTUARY
  A Man of Habit
  Church of the Moon
BOOK TWO: SEARCH AND DESTROY
  "My Black Princes"
  Castor and Pollux
BOOK THREE: BETRAYAL
  The Formal Education of an Operative
  Nemesis
BOOK FOUR: RETRIBUTION
  Furies
  Rest Homes/Going to Ground
EPILOGUE: THE SANCTION'S AFTERMATH
  Abelard and Heloise
  Under the Rose
  Redemption

The only place where the structure varies is in the epilogue, which consists of three parts, not two. There, the "falling action" portion of the plot had numerous elements that needed to be resolved, demanding three final sections. Also, within each fifty-page segment, I had smaller units that sometimes lasted for no more than a page or two. These were identified by numbers in the middle of pages, sometimes twenty within each fifty-page segment. The consequence was that the reader encountered frequent breaks, a device that made the experience easier for someone with limited attention.

Imagine that it's almost midnight. Although you go to bed tired, you decide to read for a while. You open *The Brotherhood of the Rose* to where you stopped reading the previous night. The only words on the page are BOOK FOUR: RETRIBUTION. You go to the next page and discover:

FURIES

1

Saul stared through the windshield toward a misty streetlight. His rented Citroen was parked in the middle of a line of cars along a residential street.

At this point you flip ahead (everybody does this) to see how much time the section is going to take. You're relieved to find that on the next page, sooner than expected, a second numbered section awaits you. No matter how tired you are, the chances are you'll get that far. The third numbered section is on the next page after that, an easy goal. You keep reading. The fourth numbered break comes quickly. So does the fifth. In this way, no matter your fatigue, you might go through an entire fifty-page chunk of FURIES. But then that large arc ends, and you find a new subtitle, REST HOMES/GOING TO GROUND. It's a signal to stop and get some sleep. In my later novels, the titles began to seem strained, and I abandoned them. BOOK ONE, BOOK TWO, BOOK THREE, etc., (call them parts or chapters if you like) now seem sufficient to do the job. Whatever the label, through a tactical use of structure, the single sitting of each section is more or less preserved.

If that seems too complicated, simply remember this: By subdividing your novel, by thinking of it in terms of arcs and small units within those arcs, you're not only making it easier for you to write the book; you're also making it easier for the reader to appreciate the unity of those fifty-page sections. I'm fond of using numbers to separate the small units within the sections, but you don't need to. A couple of asterisks or three double-spaced blank lines will do the same thing.

When do you know it's time to end a small unit and begin a new one? One principle would be to provide a break whenever there's an important change in locale. I don't mean just from apartment to car to lake. Within the apartment, there have probably been changes of locale also—from living room to bedroom to balcony. Don't be extreme. Don't use a new short unit if someone is merely walking from the bedroom to the living room. But suppose it's a dramatic moment. Suppose your character hides an incriminating document in the bedroom, takes a breath, and returns to the living room to convince a police officer that nothing suspicious is going on. That might be a good time to start a new short unit. It's as if the narrative itself has taken a breath. That principle works for me because by temperament I write short scenes, but if your approach is different, you should still be able to find natural shifts in your narrative that invite frequent breaks. Note how James M. Cain uses this method in his classic, *The Postman Always Rings Twice*—his scenes are amazingly short. Flip the pages. The white spaces that are a consequence of this technique jump at you.

There's one structural unit that beginning writers are fond of but that should be approached with severe caution: flashbacks. The very name indicates the problem. By definition, flashbacks impede the forward movement of the story. In all my books, I used flashbacks only a few times, the longest of which (fifty pages) is in *The Brotherhood of the Rose* when I finally reveal how the two betrayed heroes were raised in a military-style orphanage. I agonized over that flashback. Took it out. Put it back in. Took it out. Put it back in. It wasn't in the version of the manuscript that I sent to my editor. Only when he phoned me and said that he liked the book but that something was strange about the middle, as if a big chunk were missing, did I send him those pages. He insisted that they be added, and in retrospect I think he was right—the orphanage section is the bedrock of the novel. Please, be scrupulous. Unless your book is about the nature of time and/or memory, as in Faulkner's *Absalom, Absalom!*, flashbacks are a dangerous interruptive strategy. Whenever you're tempted to use one, try to find every reason in the world not to include it. More than any other part of a book's structure, a flashback needs absolute justification.

No news there. But what about short disguised flashbacks, a paragraph long, the kind where a scene begins strongly, only to be interrupted with an explanation of how the scene came to take place? "Robert shoved the door open so hard that it banged against the wall." A tense confrontation ensues. Suddenly, the author worries that the scene's abrupt opening will confuse the reader, so a belated transition is inserted.

> Ever since Robert had wakened an hour earlier, the only thing he'd thought about was telling his lawyer what he thought of him. He'd dressed in a frenzy. He'd raced out to get a taxi, his fury mounting when he was forced to rush two blocks before he found one. Sitting on the torn back seat, frustrated by seemingly countless traffic jams, he'd become even angrier. When the taxi had finally reached the brownstone, he had charged out, so consumed by rage that he hadn't even noticed the shower that drenched him. But now he felt the blessed release of grabbing his lawyer's suit coat and slamming him against a wall.

The scene then continues. Let's chart the sequence, using the elements of the triangle I discussed earlier: AB, BC, and CD. In a disguised flashback, the scene begins with rising action in the middle: BC. It then reverts to beginning exposition: AB. Finally

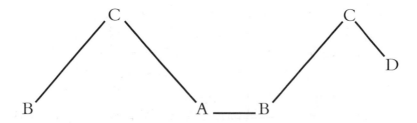

the scene is allowed to conclude: CD. Viewed in this way, the scene's construction is obviously jumbled and unsatisfying.

Nonetheless, I'm amazed how often beginning writers use that pattern. Once or twice is occasionally necessary. But for some writers, the device is as contagious as the flu. In chapter after chapter, BC is followed by AB and then jumps to CD. The repeated flawed structure causes the book to stumble. When editing your fiction, be on the lookout for scenes interrupted by a sudden string of verbs involving "had."

How do we avoid the problem? Two ways. First, this kind of flashback is usually a tacit admission by the novelist that the AB in this scene isn't an interesting way to begin so it got crammed into the middle. My response is, if it wasn't going to be interesting at the start of the scene, it certainly won't be interesting when it interrupts the main point. Unless the interruption is absolutely necessary for clarity, get rid of it. Let the reader connect the scenes for you. The second solution is to recognize that if your book has a lot of disguised flashbacks in a static situation (a character remembering the past while driving to meet someone, a character sitting in an airport, recalling conversations with someone who's about to get off a plane, or a character dreaming about the past), your plot has become tangled. If past events are so important to the story, rearrange the plot and start the book with them. Concentrate fiercely to give your plot a forward motion. You must have a powerfully necessary reason for turning it backward.

The most important structural decision you need to make involves choosing the incident with which you begin the story. Naturally, you want to use a strong event that will grab the reader's attention. But if you're not careful, you'll select a climactic event that actually belongs far along in the plot, forcing you to use flashbacks to explain who the heck these characters are and how they got into their predicament. I made this mistake in early drafts of *First Blood*, starting with Rambo being chased by the posse. He scrambled through the forest. A helicopter pursued him. He shot deputies. In theory, this approach should have guaranteed a reader's interest. But in fact, it was boring because the reader didn't know anything about Rambo and hence didn't care why the character was being chased. Worse, after all the gunplay, I then had to provide a long flashback in which quiet events explained the story's background. In an effort to avoid beginning with those quiet events, I made them seem even quieter by introducing them after a loud start. My initial draft had a massively messed up BC, AB, CD structure.

The way to avoid the problem is to ask this question during your written conversation with yourself: What is the event that sets the story into motion? This is a deceptively simple question inasmuch as the first answers are often the wrong ones. How do you know a wrong answer? It will necessitate a flashback soon after the incident you selected to start your story. Pay attention to that flashback because often *it* is the opening scene that your story wants to have. Your goal is to go back along the sequence of your plot until you find an incident that fulfils two requirements: one, it's interesting, and two, it introduces the characters without demanding a ton of background about them. Don't be over-scrupulous about this. *Every* plot requires a certain amount of background information. Otherwise, you'd need to start with a character's birth. But as long as you introduce background subtly, without a flashback, there's no problem. "Tod walked into the cocktail party, noticed the somber man drinking in the corner and thought, 'Harry still stands as if he's in uniform'." That's a reasonable, efficient way to begin. From the get-go, we meet Tod and Harry. We want to know about their relationship and what kind of uniform Harry used to wear. It's quiet, yes, but it echoes with faint thunder, implying that a lot of interesting things will soon happen.

How did I solve the problem with *First Blood*'s structure? I paid attention to the flashback that I couldn't avoid after I started the book with the chase through the mountains. Who *are* these people? I wanted to know. Where does the story really begin? The flashback kept wanting me to start with Rambo wandering into a small town and meeting its police chief. That's quiet and boring, I kept thinking. But one day, in frustration, I tried it and found that the opening grabbed me because it made me curious about the character. "His name was Rambo, and he was just some nothing kid for all anybody knew." The sentence implied that Rambo had a secret. I wanted to know what that secret was. My structural problem had been solved. The book was on its way.

A Matter of Viewpoint

As you do your research and work out the elements of plot, character, and structure, you also need to think about your story's viewpoint, the perspective from which it is told. Some writers select a viewpoint merely because it feels natural, but if you jump into a story without considering the implications of the viewpoint, you're liable to discover that your writing becomes harder as you go along. Your story may fight you until, discouraged, you abandon it, blaming the plot when actually the problem is how you're telling it. John Barth once told me that, at the start of a project, he experimented with different viewpoints to determine which of them seemed most suitable to the material. Punning, he called these various beginnings "test borings." He wanted to discover which viewpoint allowed him to get to the depth of his story and which bored him. I follow his example, evaluating the available viewpoints—omniscient, third-person limited, first person, and the rarely used second person—as if they are tools I'm setting on a table, testing and judging them.

Sometimes the selection is easy inasmuch as only one viewpoint will work for a given story. If you have a plot that shifts from locale to locale, and if each of these locales is dominated by a separate major character, it'll be a nightmare to try to narrate the story in a sequence of first persons. On rare occasions, it's been done. Faulkner's *As I Lay Dying* has fifteen first-person narrators, each of which has a distinctive tone. But Faulkner was a genius, and we'd better know what we're doing before we jump from algebra to advanced calculus. A plot with numerous major characters automatically suggests a shifting third-person point of view.

The broadest third person is omniscient—the narrator describes the events of the story from God's point of view and is able to get into the mind and emotions of any character, sometimes in the same paragraph. This all-aware narrator is able to step back and describe societies as well as sweeping historical events that none of the characters could know in the detail that the narrator provides. Victor Hugo's *Les Miserables* is a good example. The author interrupts the hunter-hunted drama between the "criminal" Valjean and his policeman pursuer, Javert, with a fifty-page overview of the Battle of Waterloo written from the perspective of a historian. He self-consciously refers to "our story" and "the reader." He's a stage manager who makes no effort to conceal himself as he manipulates the narrative. With few rules, the omniscient viewpoint is the easiest to use, but although a favorite in the nineteenth century, most authors avoid it these days because, when used in the extreme, it can distance the reader from the narrative. John ·Fowles's *The French Lieutenant's Woman*, complete with author-intruding footnotes, is an interesting modern example of this viewpoint.

The issue comes down to this: Is it possible to know what other people are thinking and feeling? Can anyone actually achieve an overview that permits an objective understanding of huge events? I have trouble understanding my own thoughts and emotions, let alone anyone else's. Each of us is limited by our perspective and biases. That's a major point of Norman Mailer's *The Armies of the Night: History as a Novel, the Novel as History*, in which Mailer recounts his personal experiences at the 1967 anti-Vietnam march on the Pentagon and then compares them to a seemingly objective overview of those same events as accumulated from newspaper reports. The two approaches offer drastically different versions of "reality."

The nineteenth century apparently felt that it was in fact possible to have objective knowledge. When Dickens begins *A Tale of Two Cities* with the general observation, "It was the best of times, it was the worst of times, it was the age of wisdom, it was the age of foolishness, it was the epoch of belief, it was the epoch of incredulity . . . " he's addressing readers who leaned toward the "belief" Dickens mentioned. His middle-class readers took for granted that absolute truth was knowable and had no difficulty accepting a world described from a cosmic perspective. But our skeptical age tends to ask, "Who's telling us this stuff about the best of times and the worst of times?" It isn't from a character's point of view. It's from the author's. No one, not even Dickens, can possibly know what's happening in England and France simultaneously and what all of those different people are thinking and feeling. *Unless this is just a made-up story.* That is the danger toward which an extreme omniscient viewpoint leads. Modern readers have a mania about credibility. To the extent that the omniscient narrator intrudes with godlike information, the illusion of actuality is broken.

An alternative is the third-person limited, a viewpoint that seems truer to life because it depicts the thoughts and feelings of only one person. The author doesn't step forward to provide information with which the viewpoint character isn't familiar. Instead, the story is channeled through that character's limited perspective. If the character doesn't know about something, the reader doesn't know about it, either. To illustrate, let's change the start of *A Tale of Two Cities* from omniscient to limited. "It was the best of times, it was the worst of times, Sydney Carton thought. He stared dismally at the date on the newspaper he was reading: 1775. The contradictions weighed on him: the age of wisdom, the age of foolishness, the season of Light, the season of Darkness. A terrifying, confusing time."

My apologies to Dickens, but I needed his help to make the point clear. In the original version, an omniscient narrator addressed the reader as an all-powerful overseer, whereas in the modified version, the reader is in one particular character's body, mind, and emotions, identifying with him. The first version is general and distanced. The second is specific and immediate. I'm not suggesting that the omniscient viewpoint is inferior to the limited one. Dickens's brilliant all-aware opening is well suited to a novel that looks back at the French Revolution with the benefit of a historical perspective not available to the people who lived through that turbulent period. What I *am* suggesting is that these two viewpoints are tools with different uses and that you can save yourself a ton of narrative heartache by assessing their pros and cons before you start your story.

In your written conversation with yourself, ask whose story you're telling. If you have several major characters who are frequently separated from each other, you probably need to structure the story so that you move back and forth among them, giving each character a distinct third-person perspective; the result is a string of limited viewpoints. It all comes down to providing information to the reader. Ask yourself, "What information is absolutely essential to the plot? What character or characters can best reveal it?" If you find that several important scenes happen off stage and that the reader only learns about these events through one character telling another about someone else, that's dull storytelling. Those important off-stage scenes need to be brought *on* stage and their viewpoint character introduced.

Sometimes, though, you *don't want* to switch to other characters. If your story is about someone's process of self-discovery, it makes sense to stay within that single character's perspective. That's what happens in James's *The Ambassadors*, the novel usually considered to be the first major use of the third-person limited viewpoint. There, a conventional, close-minded man from a straightlaced New England town journeys to Paris to try to convince the heir to a mundane manufacturing enterprise to return home and help run the family business. In the process, "the ambassador" learns to develop his awareness and appreciate his surroundings, "to live," only to find that he isn't as aware as he believed, that the young man has duped him, and that he has to sacrifice his new appreciation of life by returning to the glum town from which he came. The book's viewpoint is its theme— the limitations of individual perspective.

Whether to use a string of limited third-persons or only one can be a matter of trail and error. In *First Blood*, I initially told the story completely from Rambo's third-person limited viewpoint. But although there was a lot of action, the plot wasn't engaging. Must be a bad idea, I told myself. Never should have tried it. I put the manuscript in a drawer, but I couldn't get it out of my mind. It kept nagging at me until I tried it again, and this time I wondered if the problem wasn't the plot but rather how I was telling it. Maybe I should use another character's viewpoint, I thought. But whose? The only character of importance was Rambo, I assured myself.

But then I tested that assumption and realized that sometimes a story fails because its author takes too much for granted about it. Rambo was the only character of importance? Not necessarily. What about the police chief? When Teasle arrests Rambo, the policeman is the one who sets the plot in motion. Teasle's the antagonist, and yet I was depicting him only through Rambo's eyes. The chase through the mountains was tedious because Rambo was in conflict with a faceless enemy. What if I cut back and forth between Rambo and Teasle? I wondered. We're inside Rambo as he sets a trap. We're inside Teasle as he tries to anticipate the trap. The back-and-forth viewpoints would dramatize the conflict, I realized. Of course, I couldn't start switching viewpoints halfway through the book. For consistency, I'd need to do it from the beginning, and the moment I tried it, I suddenly regained my interest in the story.

All of us are stuck in our perspectives, limited by our biases. That turned out to be a dominant theme of *First Blood*. A policeman sees no more than a vagrant and hassles him. The vagrant sees no more than a typical hard-nosed cop and fights back. As it happens, neither character is what he seems, but they don't realize that until their limited viewpoints propel them into disaster. The novel had other contrasts: the conventional tactics of the Korean War versus the guerrilla tactics of the Vietnamese War, the conformist 1950s versus the radical 1960s, the hawks versus the doves, and the Generation Gap (don't look for any of this in the movie). By constantly alternating between Rambo and Teasle in an A, B, A, B fashion, I was able to dramatize these contrasts and make the point that our assumptions about others can be dangerous. None of the violence would have happened if Rambo and Teasle had tried to understand each other. The alternating third-person limited view-points stated these themes without needing to make them explicit. Technique became subject matter.

But there is another type of third-person viewpoint in *First Blood*, and it takes us back to Dickens. Even after I used alternating limited viewpoints to build conflict, I still felt troubled about the novel's beginning. As I mentioned in my comments about struc-ture, the initial early scenes in which Rambo came to town seemed too quiet. I was reasonably sure that I could keep the reader's interest after Rambo's jailbreak, but I kept worrying that the reader would get bored earlier and close the book. What am I going to do? I wondered. How can I assure the reader that every-thing at the start is going to pay off later, that there are plenty of exciting events about to happen? In desperation, I added the following first paragraph:

> His name was Rambo, and he was just some nothing kid for all anybody knew, standing by the pump of a gas station on the outskirts of Madison, Kentucky. He had a long heavy beard, and his hair was hanging down over his ears to his neck, and he had his hand out trying to thumb a ride from a car that was stopped at the pump. To see him there, leaning on one hip, a Coke bottle in his hand and a rolled-up sleeping bag near his boots on the tar pavement, you could never have guessed that on Tuesday, a day later, most of the police in Basalt County would be hunting him down. Certainly you could not have guessed that by Thursday he would be running from the Kentucky National Guard and the police of six counties and a good many private citizens who liked to shoot. But then from just seeing him there ragged and dusty by the pump of the gas station, you could never have figured the kind of kid Rambo was, or what was about to make it all begin.

Now who on Earth is reporting this information, and who is the "you" so frequently mentioned? This looks suspiciously like an omniscient narrator in the manner of Dickens and Hugo directly addressing the reader. The technique is intrusive. It's self-conscious. But for the life of me, I couldn't think of another way to start the narrative. Because it promises excitement, I got away with it, and because it worked for me the first time, I used a similar omniscient opening in my second novel, *Testament*, which is about a family under attack from terrorists.

> It was the last morning the four of them would ever be together: the man and his wife, his daughter and his son. The son was just a baby, the daughter still in grade school. That didn't matter. In time, nothing did. It came upon them almost comically—the man sat at the breakfast table, his bare feet on the cold hardwood floor, and glancing over by the stove, he saw the cat slump into her bowl of milk.

Again I ask, who is reporting those first few sentences? The impending disaster is not anything that the man at the breakfast table could know. The whole point of the scene is that the man is startled when the cat slumps into the bowl of milk. The "terrible things are about to happen" tone isn't from a character's viewpoint. It's from the insecure author's, trying to get the reader's attention. The device is called dramatic irony—the omniscient narrator tells the reader something that a character can't possibly know, and the reader, armed with insider information, waits with interest to learn how the character will react when he realizes what is actually going on.

Only when the man sits at the breakfast table, "his bare feet on the cold hardwood floor," do we shift from an omniscient to a limited viewpoint, feeling with the character as he glances toward the stove and sees the cat slump into the milk. If I could write that sentence anew, I'd have the man "glancing to the right toward the stove," making the limited viewpoint more immediate by putting the reader into the man's spatial perspective. In fact, now that I think about it, the majority of my novels begin with some sort of omniscient voice, either in the form of a magazine article (*Burnt Sienna*) or as a mysterious historical prologue (*The Brotherhood of the Rose* trilogy). But later sections are told from limited perspectives. Immediately after the omniscient opening paragraph of *First Blood*, for instance, the focus shifts exclusively to what Rambo sees, feels, and thinks.

> Rambo knew there was going to be trouble, though. Big trouble, if somebody didn't watch out. The car he was trying to thumb a ride with nearly ran him over when it left the pump. The station attendant crammed a charge slip and a book of trade stamps into his pocket and grinned at the tire marks on the hot tar close to Rambo's feet. Then the police car pulled out of traffic toward him and he recognized the start of the pattern again and stiffened. "No, by God, not this time. This time I won't be pushed."

We're inside Rambo's perspective instead of being told about him from a distance.

So what lessons did I learn? That the omniscient viewpoint is risky because it's intrusive and lacks immediacy, but sometimes it can't be avoided. Use it sparingly, only at the start, seldom after that, but if you begin with a limited viewpoint, you can never break that viewpoint by switching to an omniscient voice later in the story. In the post-Victorian era, one of the few rationales I can imagine for writing a narrative entirely in the omniscient voice is that the story pretends to be some sort of researched history. I did this in *Last Reveille*, a novel about America's military invasion of Mexico to hunt the Mexican bandit Pancho Villa after his raid on an American border town. That book's historian narrator provides maps, gives quotations from other historians, and frequently interrupts the narrative with informative asides. My assumption was that the reader would be so interested in the surprising historical facts that the intrusive viewpoint wouldn't be a distraction. Indeed, the intrusive narrator was the reason the book was written. But apart from that special justification for a book-long omniscient narrator, I'm wary of it.

Third-person limited. By default, that's the viewpoint I prefer. If you're good at role-playing, if you can imagine you are inside a character, if you can think and feel with that character and make your readers share those thoughts and feelings, you can trap your readers and make them feel they're inside the story instead of merely reading it.

Before we proceed to the other major viewpoint—the first person—let's look briefly at the seldom-used second person. As an experiment, I employed it in a novella "The Beautiful Uncut Hair of Graves," which begins like this:

> Despite the rain, you've been to the cemetery yet again, ignoring the cold autumn gusts slanting under your bowed umbrella, the drenched drab leaves blowing against your soaked pant legs and shoes.
>
> Two graves. You shiver, blinking through tears toward the freshly laid sod. There aren't any tombstones. There won't be for a year. But you imagine what the markers will look like.

In psychiatric terms, people who refer to themselves as "you" are disassociating from themselves. Thus one effect of this passage is that it distances the reader. But because the passage also uses the present tense, there's a second and contradictory effect of drawing the reader in. My justification for this approach was that the main character is in a state of shock and grief. The second-person view-point, I reasoned, would approximate the detached way the trau-matized main character sees himself. At the same time, I wanted the present tense to communicate the immediacy of his pain.

The best-known book-length example of the second person is Jay McInerney's *Bright Lights, Big City*. McInerney combines the second-person viewpoint with the present tense, also, thus taking the reader both out of and into the story simultaneously. The effect is to communicate the main character's mental and emotional

imbalance as cocaine controls his life. He's detached from everything except his drug experiences.

> You start to laugh. She laughs too. You slap your thigh. She wants
> to know how it's going. A very funny question. Hilarious. Amanda
> is a riot. You are laughing so hard that you choke.

Don't use this complex technique unless you're totally
convinced that the nature of your story demands it. Employing
it once in a career is plenty. Be prepared for a critical backlash.
Some readers will find the approach so off-putting that they'll
call it a gimmick.

With that controversial viewpoint out of the way, let's proceed
to one so complicated and dangerous that it deserves a lesson all
to itself: the seductive first person and the narrative heartbreak it
can cause.

The First Person

ℯ

O n the surface, the first person seems the simplest of all viewpoints. Write the way you talk, the siren song says. Just let the words come out as if the story were happening to you. Unfortunately, a transcription of even the best oral story-telling proves that what sounds effective in a casual across-the-table setting is wordy and ill-focused on a page. Compounding the problem, authors who reflexively choose the first person often forget that they're trying to create fictional characters. These authors identify so closely with their first-person narrators that they take for granted the vividness of the language they're using. Neglecting to include the details of sound, touch, taste, and smell that make a story palpable, they rely almost exclusively on details of sight, with the result that their prose has a one-dimensional quality. The sentences can become a litany of I did this and I did that and I did something else until the reader is overwhelmed with egotism and closes the pages.

But laziness of language isn't the only temptation the first person offers. It also encourages laziness of dramatic context. If the first person were as easy as it seems, all stories would be written in that viewpoint. The reason they're not has nothing to do with the need for variety. Rather it's that not many stories *are suited* to the first person. Form should follow function. Viewpoint should have something to do with the narrative's theme. An author shouldn't choose a first-person viewpoint unless no other viewpoint will work, unless there is something unique to the first person that permits an author to create an effect that couldn't be achieved any other way.

Here's an example of a well-known novel whose first person I think is ill-chosen and works against the story's drama. The book is *Deliverance*, its author the poet James Dickey. The plot concerns a group of four male friends who take a canoe trip down a wild river in a remote section of the American South. On the second day, they're assaulted by back-country woodsmen. After a harrowing ordeal in which members of both sides are killed, the surviving main characters barely escape to a town on the edge of the wilderness. There, a police chief becomes suspicious about what happened along the river, but the main characters can't tell him, afraid that relatives of the woodsmen they killed will want revenge or that the local law won't understand that the killings were in self-defense. So the survivors claim a boating accident drowned one of their group and badly injured another. At last the policeman stops asking questions and lets them return to civilization.

The point here is that the survivors can't let anyone know what happened on that river. Otherwise, the relatives of the woodsmen will stalk them. There's only one problem. The book is narrated in the first person by one of the survivors, a graphics consultant named Ed. If it's so important to keep the secret, why did Ed write about what happened, emphasizing that no one can ever know about it? I can understand that a man in his position might keep a secret account so that his memory would be fresh if the law came for him. But wouldn't he hide the document? Why do I have this book in my hand? How did his first-person account become public? I was hooked until the end when the lack of justification for the first person ruined the book for me. Nothing would have been lost if the novel had been told in the limited third person, from the viewpoint of the same character who now narrates it, but something *was* lost by using the first person. There was no reason to use it but a good reason not to. It always seemed to me that Dickey chose that viewpoint because its emotive possibilities attracted him as a poet. In other words, it felt natural. Again, that dangerous siren song.

By contrast, here's a story in which the first person is used brilliantly. In fact, it's the most famous instance of the first person I can think of: Henry James's horror novel, *The Turn of the Screw*. Its main character is a young English governess hired by a handsome aristocrat to take care of his dead brother's niece and nephew on his remote country estate. After the aristocrat leaves for business in London, the governess starts noticing shadowy figures on the property. Puzzled, she describes these figures to a servant and learns that the figures resemble a man and woman, Peter Quint and Miss Jessel, lovers, who used to work on the estate. But of course it couldn't have been them, the servant explains, because the man and the woman are dead now. Nonetheless, the governess sees more of these apparitions until she becomes afraid that she's seeing ghosts, that the spirits of the dead lovers have returned from the grave to possess the children and continue their love affair.

In desperation, the governess decides that the children will be safer if they're separated. She sends the little girl away and keeps the boy under her own protection. When Quint appears at a window, the governess defies the apparition, shouting that the boy is hers. The boy cries out like "a creature hurled over an abyss . . . I caught him, yes, I held him—it may be imagined with what a passion; but at the end of a minute I began to feel what it truly was that I held. We were alone with the quiet day, and his little heart, dispossessed, had stopped."

Thus *The Turn of the Screw* ends, and in the more than a century since it was written, that final scene continues to provoke discussion. What happened? Did the boy die of fright? Or did the governess succeed in repelling Quint but the shock of being dispossessed killed the child? With no neat resolution, the story has disturbed many readers, often leading them to conclude that there is more to the story than is first apparent. James hinted as much when he called *The Turn of the Screw* "a trap for the unwary," "a piece of ingenuity pure and simple, of cold artistic calculation . . . to catch those not easily caught." But caught in what way?

The story's textual history perhaps gives a clue. Ten years after its 1898 publication, James included it in a monumental collection of his work. But now the story was changed. Perhaps wanting to give away his secret, James made the governess's verbs of perception less definitive. Instead of saying that she saw a figure on a parapet, she now stated that she *seemed* to see a figure on the parapet. Other sightings of the "ghosts" were qualified in a similar fashion. She *appeared* to see a figure near a pond. "I saw" became "I felt." What are we to make of the changes? Did she or did she not see Quint and Miss Jessel? Over the years, scholars debated the issue, and the most intriguing conclusion is that the governess was mentally unbalanced. Young and inexperienced, on her first job away from home, she fell in love with the handsome aristocrat who hired her. When he left the estate, she transferred the passion she felt for him to the children. She subconsciously hoped that, if the children were in danger and she protected them like a mother, she could so impress the aristocrat that he would marry her. Further, the tactic of separating the children gave her the chance to be alone with the astonishingly attractive boy, a surrogate for the aristocrat. When she held the boy "with what a passion," she squeezed the life from him. The malign force in the story wasn't Quint or Miss Jessel, but the governess, who hadn't the faintest idea of what she had done.

The Turn of the Screw will sustain this interpretation just as it will sustain an interpretation as a straight ghost story. Because of the use of the first person, we'll never know, and for me, that makes the story all the more intriguing—the wonderful way that a skillful use of the first person can entangle a reader. In that respect, when James spoke of "a trap for the unwary," he was referring to his use of the first person as much as he was to the events of the narrative. After all, as in any superbly told story, the viewpoint can't be separated from the plot. Whenever I read a first-person narrative, I always ask myself, "Who's telling me these events? Is the narrator reliable?" Certainly, if someone came to me in real life and told me this story, I'd be foolish not to be skeptical. Yet on the page it's eerily believable. This led James to suggest that the few legitimate reasons for using the first person involved character studies in which the narrator was either self-deluded, a liar, a fool, or insane. His point was that, if the reader believes a first-person story without paying attention to its teller, the reader isn't only naive but misses most of the enjoyment of the tale. *The Turn of the Screw* can't work, except in the first person. That's the test. Can you change a story from the first person to the third person without losing anything? If so, the odds are that the story shouldn't be in the first person.

Granted, James was being too restrictive. I can think of novels in which I accept the first-person narrator's reliability without much question: *The Great Gatsby*, for example. Because of the title, some readers mistakenly believe that Fitzgerald's novel is about Gatsby whereas it's actually about the narrator, Nick Carraway, who tells us how his life changed because of his encounter with Gatsby, how a seemingly special man was actually a bootlegger and how the shallow rich people he hung around with made a mess of other people's lives. Given this tactic (a loss-of-illusions memoir from Carraway's point of view), there's no other way to tell the story. To make sure that the reader trusted the first-person narrator, Fitzgerald took pains to have Carraway begin his story by insisting that he's a tolerant and objective observer, hence presumably trust-worthy. Even then, an attentive reader has to accept that Carraway's self-admitted need to stand at "moral attention forever" will inevitably color his version of the disastrous events.

Another famous first-person narrative, Twain's *Adventures of Huckleberry Finn,* is a memoir in which Huck tells us about the beatings and corpses and murders he saw as he drifted along the Mississippi. I believe what he tells me. I find the slang of his account totally engaging. But the third person can be believable and use slang as well, so the question becomes, could Twain's book have worked just as effectively in the third person? To find out, let's look at Twain's parallel effort, *The Adventures of Tom Sawyer,* which has a third-person viewpoint. To me, there's no contest. *Tom Sawyer* is all on the surface, a one-thing-after-another boy's adventure narrative, full of incidents that captivate the reader the first time but bring no surprises on second reading.

In contrast, *Huckleberry Finn* is more powerful because Huck's first-person narrative subconsciously reveals how traumatized the boy is. Huck tells his story as if it's a joke, but the alert reader understands that the boy's humor is a protective mechanism, that he is so horrified by the atrocities he experienced along the river that he's close to a mental collapse. As Huck eventually admits, "I ain't a-going to tell *all* that happened—it would make me sick again to do that. I wished I hadn't ever come ashore that night to see such things. I ain't ever going to get shut of them—lots of times I dream about them." The contrast between Huck's usually humorous tone (a defensive one) and his dark subject are what make the first-person work here. The "I" narrator also gains depth because Huck is so naive that the reader often understands events better than Huck does. For more on this, read Philip Young's "Adventures of Huckleberry Finn" in *Ernest Hemingway: A Reconsideration*.

The same can be said about J. D. Salinger's *The Catcher in the Rye*, in which the narrator's use of humor disguises his nervous breakdown (he's telling his story to a psychiatrist). In the best writing, the first person implies an unstated deeper level, a hidden lower layer of character revelation, that the first person isn't aware of and that the third person wouldn't be able to create. That point is worth emphasizing—when skillfully used, the "I" narrator often doesn't understand the true nature of what he or she is saying. It's up to the reader to figure it out. But if there *isn't* anything to figure out, if the first-person account is all surface, the reader will tire of a one-dimensional I-I-I and go somewhere else.

If you do decide that your story is one of those rare instances in which the first person is legitimately required, you still need to find a reason for the story to be in the reader's hands. Unless your narrator is a professional writer, it would take a long time for the first person to write the account. For that matter, even professional writers can take a long time. So your character better have a damned good reason for struggling so long to write the story. A psychological trauma is a common explanation. Something so awful happened that the character felt driven to sit down and write about it, or *talk* about it as in Conrad's *Heart of Darkness*, an interesting example because it's a first-person narrative transmitted by another first person.

Why did the narrator of *The Turn of the Screw* write her story? The ever-diligent James is careful to supply an opening chapter in which guests at a country mansion exchange eerie stories. One of the guests, an unnamed first person, introduces a manuscript written by the governess, who had died twenty years earlier. To the end of her life, it seems, the governess was so troubled by the events she experienced that she felt compelled to put them on paper. As a bonus, this first-person-within-a-first-person technique not only justifies the existence of the manuscript but provides a context of a misty past that makes the story more atmospheric and believable. A good way to test if the first-person was ill-chosen is to ask yourself, "Why is this character telling me this?" If there's no necessary reason or if the answer is contradictory to the narrative's logic ("no one must ever know my secret"), you're in the wrong viewpoint, and it's time to switch to the third person.

Perhaps the most common use of the first person is in detective stories. For the most part, this is a convention that has lapsed into cliche. Edgar Allan Poe, the inventor of the detective story, established this first-person tradition in "The Murders in the Rue Morgue" (1841). The exploits of his French detective, C. Auguste Dupin, are seen through the eyes of a friend. Sir Arthur Conan Doyle later borrowed this device, narrating the adventures of Sherlock Holmes through the first-person viewpoint of Dr. Watson. In America, in the 1920s, *Black Mask* magazine favored getting rid of the sideline narrator and letting the fictional detective tell what happened, presumably for the detective's files. The ultimate result was the glory of first-person detective narrators, Raymond Chandler's Philip Marlowe.

Since then, it seems that every beginning detective-story writer chooses the first person by default and almost always looks like an imitator. Chandler had a unique sense of tone especially suited for his first-person approach. Even the best of his inheritors, Ross Macdonald for example, couldn't achieve the charm of Chandler's prose, largely because the first person is only as interesting as the character telling the story and the fictional Philip Marlowe has personality to burn while Macdonald's Lew Archer by and large only gives us information. What is arguably the greatest American detective novel, Dashiell Hammett's *The Maltese Falcon*, is a *third-person* narrative. With that in mind, I recommend that anyone planning to write a detective story recognize the overdone first-person viewpoint and avoid it. Innovate instead of imitate. At the least, make sure that your first-person detective has a reason, other than convention, to narrate the story.

Sometimes a first-person narrator is necessary if your viewpoint character is so off-putting that the reader won't want to read the story without the identification that the intimate first person provides. My favorite example is James M. Cain's *The Postman Always Rings Twice*. A hard-boiled novel that depicts a murderous love triangle set in Los Angeles during the Depression, the book has the exemplary first sentence, "They threw me off the hay truck about noon." Who is the narrator? What was he doing on the hay truck? Why did they throw him off? The opening is so stark, with so many implied questions, that I'm compelled to keep reading, to learn more. Cain writes so economically and vividly that he avoids the flat effect of many first-person accounts. The egotistical I-I-I that makes many first-person stories wearying is a plus here, for it perfectly depicts the selfish nature of the main character, who kills the husband of the woman he lusts after. Hard times like the Depression turn people into animals, Cain seems to say. Or maybe the narrator of the novel was born that way. There aren't any absolute answers, but because the reader is in the head and heart of the killer, a repulsive character becomes understandable and compelling. Conscientious writer that he is, Cain follows the rules and takes care to provide a reason for the first-person account to exist. The narrator is writing it as a confession before he goes to the gas chamber. The account was presumably later published as a cautionary illustration of what happens when dark emotions control us.

But how many explanations can there be for why a first-person account came to be written and how the manuscript arrived in the reader's hands? I wrote a lot of first-person short stories, and after a while, the few justifications I could imagine for why the narrator takes the time to sit down and write the story began to seem wearying and repetitious. For believability, the existence of the first-person manuscript needed to be accounted for, I felt, and yet I'd reached a dead end in terms of making the explanation various and interesting. Then I remembered Robert Browning's poetic use of a form called the dramatic monologue, and I had a breakthrough. Borrowed from stage drama, the dramatic mono-logue is basically a first-person account that a character delivers to an invisible listener. In the process, the narrator reveals more personal characteristics than he intends to.

Browning's best-known example, "My Last Duchess," begins,

> That's my last Duchess painted on the wall,
> Looking as if she were alive. I call
> That piece a wonder, now: Fra Pandolf's hands
> Worked busily a day, and there she stands.
> Will't please you sit and look at her?

The narrator tells his unidentified listener the story of the marriage and how he got tired of his wife's easygoing manner with other men.

> Oh, Sir, she smiled, no doubt
> Whene'er I passed her; but who passed without
> Much the same smile? This grew; I gave commands;
> Then all smiles stopped together.

For a stark moment, the reader wonders about the implication of what the narrator has just said. He gave commands? All smiles stopped? Did he have her killed? Does he bring visitors to his art gallery to admire a trophy painting of the beautiful murdered woman who was once his wife? It's a horrifying situation in which the reader (as invisible listener) is shocked by the portrait while the narrator is proud of the painting and thinks that what he did to his wife was justifiable.

This dramatic monologue meets many of the requirements for the first person as I admire it. First, it *needs* to be in the first person. The effect is created because of the contrast between the first-person's attitude and the reader's attitude. The "I" thinks it's normal, but *we're* appalled. This extra level (who's telling this and how would I react if I heard this in real life?) provides the kind of dimension the best first persons have. Second, Browning gives an explanation for the existence of the narrative—a duke is telling a visitor about his dead wife.

That last point might seem obvious, but for me it was the breakthrough I mentioned. I'd been so fixated on providing an explanation for why the first person wrote the story and how the reader came into contact with it that I hadn't considered an alternative that we encounter every day in life. People constantly tell us stories. They don't write them down. They just tell us. So, as a writer, why couldn't I pretend that I was in a bar, say, or that I'd met a stranger waiting for a bus or that I was sitting next to somebody on a plane, and that person said, as strangers sometimes do, "You know the damnedest thing just happened to me." Or maybe it's a friend who's saying this. Whoever, that person becomes like Coleridge's ancient mariner and blurts out the story while I listen aghast. This is the approach Conrad uses in *Heart of Darkness* and, arguably, Fitzgerald in *The Great Gatsby*.

I can't tell you how liberating that thought was. I didn't need to imagine my narrator writing frantically for a month or a year. I didn't need to account for the written document, only the tale itself. With that condition loosened, stories came more easily.

How did these supposedly oral stories get transcribed into print? I have no idea, but I make that leap of faith when I read "My Last Duchess," so I hope that, if my dramatic monologues are gripping enough, readers will grant the same concession to me.

Still, there's a big difference between a dramatic monologue that occupies thirty pages and one that occupies four hundred. After writing a hundred pages of a first-person novel, I find the viewpoint limiting. Another character's perspective begins to seem more interesting. I want to switch to it, something easily done in the third person but not in the first. In fact, I can think of only a handful of examples that manage to switch viewpoints within a first-person context. In *Bleak House*, Dickens alternates the first person with the third-person omniscient. In *The Sound and the Fury*, Faulkner uses three first persons of increasing mental age, then concludes the novel with an omniscient third person. In *As I lay Dying*, Faulkner mixes *fifteen* first-person narrators. In Emily Bronte's *Wuthering Heights*, an "I" narrator on the Yorkshire moors records a series of first-person accounts that the locals tell about the doomed lovers, Heathcliff and Cathy. In other words, first person within first person. I can justify these complex approaches. As should always be the case with unusual techniques, they aren't gratuitous. But it would take a lot of pages to explain why they work, and unless you're awfully sure of yourself, I recommend that you master the basics of the first person before ignoring them.

Let me tell you what it was like for me after three decades of writing third-person novels to do a book in the first-person. As mentioned, several of my short stories are dramatic monologues in the manner of Browning. Indeed, my first professional sale was a first-person short story called "The Dripping," which *Ellery Queen's Mystery Magazine* bought for the lavish sum of $100 in 1971. It began:

> That autumn, we live in a house in a village, my mother's house, the house I was raised in. I have been to the village, struck even more by how nothing in it has changed and yet everything has, because I am older now, seeing it differently. I feel as though I am both here now and back then, at once with the mind of a boy and a man.

The story ends with the exact same paragraph. I wanted to create the effect that the intervening horrifying events had so traumatized the narrator that he would be eternally trapped in a constant present tense of his mind, forever resuffering what he had seen and done. In short, I had a reason for choosing the viewpoint. In three thousand words, I didn't feel its limitation. Later, in stories of six thousand or even twelve thousand words, I still didn't feel confined. But I tried at least six of my novels in the first person, each time giving up in frustration once I got deeply into the story.

The problem, in part, had to do with the nature of what I write: thrillers. Some critics argue that the first person is wrong for that kind of novel because a first-person viewpoint removes suspense, telling the reader from the start that the narrator survived all the threats against him. My favorite thriller novelist, Geoffrey Household (*Rogue Male* and *Watcher in the Shadows*), tried getting around this problem by sometimes putting a document at the start of a book, a letter from a lawyer or some such, telling the reader that the man who wrote the book is now dead and that it's important for his document to be made public. As a consequence, a degree of suspense was created by making the reader wonder not *whether* the main character was going to die but *how* it was going to happen.

But this is a special solution that draws attention to the problem as much as it solves it. In fact, over the years, the more I thought about whether suspense and the first person were incompatible in thrillers, the more I came to believe it's a false issue. Let's assume that I convert a first-person thriller into the third-person limited. The reader still follows the same single character as the hero confronts various dangers. After three hundred pages of the same third-person limited viewpoint, the reader would be infuriated if I suddenly had that character shot to death and out of the blue introduced a totally new third-person limited narrator.

The only viewpoints I can use if I intend to kill a main character two thirds of the way through a novel are third-person omniscient or *multiple* third-person limited viewpoints that have been established early in the book. In *The Brotherhood of the Rose*, I killed a main character, Chris, two-thirds of the way through. I could do that only because I had *three* third-person limited viewpoints in that book and thus had two to take up the slack when the third disappeared. But when a book's viewpoint is restricted to one character, whether in the first person or the third-person limited, the same lack of suspense applies in terms of whether or not that character will die. To me, it's one of the rare cases where first person and third person aren't different.

So I lost my overscrupulous attitude about the first person when it came to thrillers. Feeling a little more free, I had an idea that I thought would be suitable for that viewpoint. Twenty-five years ago, there were two brothers: Brad, age thirteen, and Petey, age nine. Petey followed Brad everywhere until finally, in a fit of annoyance, Brad told Petey to get lost, which is exactly what happened—Petey bicycled away and was never seen again. Brad never stopped blaming himself.

Now Brad is a successful architect who specializes in houses that blend so well with their environment that they're almost invisible. The effect is so eerie that in Denver, where he lives, the CBS television station does a news segment about him, mentioning that Brad's brother Petey disappeared when they were children. Suddenly, various men appear, claiming to be Petey. Brad quickly exposes them as imposters. But one man knows so many intimate details about Petey that Brad is overwhelmingly convinced and welcomes his long-lost brother, who painfully explains that for six years a man and a woman kept him prisoner and abused him in an underground room. After Petey finally escaped, he never went home because he'd been brainwashed into believing that Petey's mother and father would be ashamed of him.

Brad, Petey, and Brad's young son Jason go on a camping trip into the Rockies. They climb to a bluff and admire the mountains. Jason goes shyly around a boulder to urinate. Brad continues to admire the scenery. Whump! Pushed by Petey, Brad suddenly plummets off the bluff and survives only because he lands on a ledge. It takes him three days to struggle back to civilization, by which time he discovers that Petey has kidnapped both Jason and Brad's wife, Kate. To make matters worse, the FBI uses fingerprints to determine that the man who called himself Petey is actually Lester Dant, a career criminal who presumably crossed paths with Petey and learned enough to fool Brad. But Brad isn't convinced. The details the kidnapper told him about Petey's youth were too specific. Moreover, he fears that, if the FBI is correct, Lester Dant is the kind of man who would kill Jason and Kate after he got tired of abusing them. In contrast, Petey would keep them alive because he wants to take Brad's place and have the wife and son Brad prevented him from having.

A year passes. The FBI investigation fails. In desperation, Brad sets out to try to find his wife and son, to track down Petey or whoever it was that abducted his family, and . . .

At this point, I asked myself what viewpoint would be suitable. Most kidnapping novels have multiple third-person viewpoints: the victim, the criminal, the investigator, and the husband or wife whose fear worsens as the investigation goes nowhere. The novel crosscuts among them as tension increases.

But is there another way to tell the story? Since multiple third-person viewpoints are the predictable way a kidnapping story is developed, I considered the alternatives: first person and a single third-person viewpoint. There wasn't any doubt that the viewpoint character would be Brad. The issue was how to present him: "I" or "he."

I finally settled on the first person because I wanted the reader to be directly in the agony of Brad's mind, without any buffers, knowing only what Brad knew, experiencing his pain first hand. While another novelist might cut to the kidnapper and what was happening to Kate and Jason, to me that shift of scene was unrealistic because in life that's what Brad would be most frantic to know and exactly what he *couldn't* know. Brad's terrible lack of knowledge was, for me, the core of the novel. The first person—which is the most trapped of viewpoints—seemed to me the ideal way to dramatize what interested me most about Brad's character. The book would be called *Long Lost*, and the viewpoint would demonstrate that Brad was as lost as his family, as lost as his brother, Petey, had ever been.

So far so good, I thought. The opening pages came without difficulty, quickly establishing the novel's context. To make a point, I'll quote the first paragraph.

> When I was a boy, my kid brother disappeared. Vanished from the face of the earth. His name was Petey, and he was bicycling home from an after-school baseball game. Not that he'd been playing. The game was for older guys like me, which is to say that I was all of thirteen and Petey was only nine. He thought the world of me; he always wanted to tag along. But the rest of the guys complained that he was in the way, so I told Petey to "get lost, go home." I still remember the hurt look he gave me before he got on his bike and pedaled away, a skinny little kid with a brushcut, glasses, braces on his teeth, and freckles, wearing a droopy T-shirt, baggy jeans, and sneakers—the last I saw of him. That was twenty-five years ago. Yesterday.

My reason for quoting the paragraph is this: The novel has a first-person narrator, but only one sentence in this long example begins with the word "I." In fact, the word "I" is used only five times. Other first-person indicators such as "me" and "my" are used even less, respectively only three times and once. The paragraph was carefully modified to avoid the obvious liability of the first person, the nagging narcissistic I-I-I of it.

Deliberately, I continued in this manner, wanting the benefit of the first person without its baggage. I even decided how the document came into existence; under a psychiatrist's care, Brad is writing a journal, struggling to come to terms with the hell he's been through. I reached the hundred-page mark, which is usually a major obstacle. Got past it. Reached *two* hundred pages and passed *that* road block. Began to feel that, after six previous attempts to write a novel in the first person, I was finally going to succeed. And then . . . And then . . .

The entire enterprise sagged to a halt because I finally was forced to admit that I'd fallen into the trap of allowing the first person to control me instead of the other way around. I'd started writing the way I spoke. I'd started telling rather than showing. I'd started yammering instead of getting to the point. Here's an example of what I mean. It was mercifully cut from the finished book. At the time, I was so trapped in the yak-yak-yak of the first person that I didn't realize how unnecessary this material was. God bless you for wading through it. The context is that Brad has finally decided to hunt his brother (if the man in fact *is* his brother). Brad's desperate tactic is to try to reconstruct the kidnapper's logic, to put himself in "Petey's" mind.

> The idea didn't come to me as abruptly as it sounds. Not only Christmas and New Year's had passed, but also Kate's birthday, my birthday, and Petey's birthday. Winter had given way to spring. My efforts to investigate through the Internet had led nowhere, and as the one-year mark of the abductions neared, helplessness tore me apart. It was increasingly clear that the police and the FBI had given up. Jesus, there had to be something I could do to find them, I thought.
>
> A year earlier, when I'd told Kate's parents what had happened, they'd wanted to rush to Denver. My response had been that they should stay where they were, that they weren't going to accomplish anything by leaving their home. Now it was my turn to want to rush somewhere. I felt an irresistible urge to get on the road, to search.
>
> My efforts would normally have been aimless. The difference was that I kept thinking about the bond between brothers, about the genes that Petey and I shared. I remembered a conversation I'd had with Kate about how twins separated at birth and reunited as adults often discovered that they dressed the same and thought the same, had similar jobs and similar-looking wives, etc. Kate had reminded me that Petey and I weren't twins, that I shouldn't expect a lot of similarity. Certainly the opposite paths that Petey and I had taken proved her right. And yet I couldn't help focusing on how

savagely Petey wanted to become me, even to the point of abducting my family. If I could imagine his thought processes, if I could reconstruct his logic, I might be able to find where he'd taken Kate and Jason. It was desperation, I knew, but at least it would be motion.

It would keep me sane.

By then, the anniversary of the abductions loomed. The start of the sequence was the second Wednesday of June. I went down to the street where Petey had first approached me when I came out of my office. The time was shortly after 2 p.m., as it had been a year earlier.

The best thing I can say about these paragraphs is that only three sentences begin with "I." Some of you might say, "I don't get it. What's wrong with them?" If so, I recommend that you stay away from the first person. What's wrong is that nothing is happening here. There's not one palpable detail. Nothing is dramatized. It's all summary and explanation. To borrow a metaphor from the broadcasting industry, it's all dead air. I know how to write better than this, so I can only conclude that the siren song of the viewpoint seduced me into merrily writing page after page of this stuff without realizing that it was flat.

When I'm preparing a first draft, I rewrite in small chunks at the beginning of each session. Thus, in this case, only when I began reading the manuscript as a whole, getting an overview, planning a more polished version, did I realize the trouble I was in. Dear Lord, how am I going to fix this? I thought. What confused me more than anything was that I felt I knew how to handle the first person because of all the short stories that I'd written from that viewpoint. Had I suddenly forgotten how to do it? What in heaven's name was my problem?

After much angst, I finally determined what was wrong. While one of the several liabilities of the first person is its tendency to encourage a writer to jabber away, the necessary compression of a short story had compensated, putting the controls on the narrator's motor mouth. But in the first draft of *Long Lost*, I was thinking like a novelist, not a short-story writer. I was aiming toward expansion, not compression. As a consequence, I had unwittingly let the first-person narrator run wild. In my second draft, I cut as if working on a short story. I took out chunks and chunks of summary and explanation, getting quickly to dramatized scenes and palpable details, showing, not telling. This is the final revised version of the wordy paragraphs you read a while ago.

> Put myself in Petey's mind? Think like him? It was desperation, yes, but what was the alternative? At least it would be motion. It would keep me from losing my own mind. I went to the street where Petey had first approached me outside my office. The time was shortly after 2 p.m., as it had been exactly a year earlier. Petey had shouted my name from behind me, which meant that he'd been waiting to the left of the building's revolving door. I walked to a large concrete flower planter, where I guessed that he'd been resting his hips. I studied the front door, trying to put myself in his place.

Now you're in a scene. Something is happening. The words don't get in the way. Instead they move things along.

It's a cautionary lesson. Having been through this turmoil, I think I'll stick to using the first person only in short stories while reserving the third person for my novels. Unless (this scares me, but it's also the final test) . . . unless I get an idea for a novel that can only best be told in the first person. I'll search for every reason not to use it. I'll need to be dragged kicking and screaming into using it. But if it's the only way to bring out the core of the book's essential drama, I won't have a choice: I'll do it.

The First Page

❧

Y ou've done your research. You've made decisions about structure and viewpoint. Now it's time to write the first sentence, the first paragraph, the first page . . .

At this moment, if your stomach shivers and your mind balks with indecision, don't worry—it's natural. It happens to me at the start of every project. No matter how many years I've been writing, I still need to remind myself that this is only my first draft and that it's okay to make mistakes. I'll make hundreds of corrections before I'm ready to submit the manuscript. For now, all that matters is surrendering to the idea and getting those initial words on the page.

Do I know how the plot is going to end before I start writing? Only to a limited extent. Yes, I have a basic sense of how everything will proceed, but I don't know many specifics, and I prefer it that way. After all, the reason I'm writing is that an idea for a story has possessed me and I have an uncontrollable urge to dramatize it. In effect, I'm telling the story to myself. I'm eager to learn how it turns out. If I knew all the details, if there wasn't the possibility of surprises, I'd soon get bored.

I once had an idea for a novel's opening that so excited me I started writing without any sense of its middle and end. The book was called *The Fraternity of the Stone*, and to this day I'm amused when I think of the book's setup. A mysterious man whom we know nothing about except that he has a deadly past and that his name is Drew MacLane has taken refuge in a hermit monastery in Vermont. He lives alone in a spartan room. His only contact with the outside world is a slot through which an unseen person slides a tray of food each day. For six years, he has used this deprivation to try to atone for unnamed violent sins that he committed.

The only thing that makes Drew feel human is a mouse that comes to visit him. Drew names him Stuart Little (from E. B. White's story). Each day, he gives the mouse a piece of bread. As the novel begins, Drew tosses a crust to Stuart, then closes his eyes and prays before eating. When he opens his eyes, he looks down at Stuart, surprised to find the mouse on its side, unmoving.

Drew stares at the dead mouse for several long seconds. Was Stuart old? Did he have a sudden heart attack? Drew considers that as a possibility, keeps staring at the dead mouse, and finally looks from the bread Stuart was eating to the bread that he himself was about to eat. Instincts that he struggled to subdue for the previous six years take control. Wracked by conflicting emotions, he stands, approaches the door to the outside corridor, breaks his hermit's vow, leaves his cell, and discovers that the entire monastery has been poisoned, the kitchen staff shot to death.

As an execution team searches each cell, Drew fights his way out of the monastery and vows to learn who ordered the attack. After six years of atonement, he's forced to use his hated former skills, entering an alien world in which everything seems a threat. Drew and I both faced that alien world together. I had no idea what he would do next, where he would go, what contacts from his previous life he would ask for help. I smiled when I wondered what Drew's reaction would be to learning who was president and all the other cultural changes that had occurred. I couldn't wait to go with him on his quest.

Eventually, one idea led to another, and soon I realized how *The Fraternity of the Stone* would end. But on page one, all I had was my enthusiasm for the novel's initial scenes. For other books, I've had a definite idea from the start about how they needed to proceed. Every instance is different. Each first page is a new adventure. Let your enthusiasm be your guide.

A few general rules should be followed, however. They all involve the people who'll be reading your story. I'm not talking about a mythical ideal reader, not your spouse, not your best friend, not the members of your writing group. When you start your first sentence, your first paragraph, your first page, the readers you need to keep in mind are your agent and your editor. (In a later lesson, I'll deal with the process of getting an agent. For now, pretend you have one.) If you believe what you see in the movies, agents and editors have bushels of time to conduct fascinating discussions with authors, tell them how brilliant they are, and generally be sensitive and literary. Sometimes, they have editing pencils stuck behind their ears. Almost always, they carry little bitty manuscripts that look suspiciously like the 115-page script for the movies in which they're impersonating agents or editors. They spend a lot of time at book-publishing parties and glamorous luncheons.

When people in the book business see this nonsense on the screen, they shake their head in dismay or weep with laughter. Parties? Gala publishing events? Ha. Let me tell you about an editor I know. He's around forty. He has a wife and three children. He lives in Westchester County (to raise his kids away from New York City). He gets up at 5:30 a.m., exercises, dresses, catches a ninety-minute train into the city, arrives at his office around 8:30, and has staff meetings all morning. Covers need to be chosen. Budgets must be decided. The next year's publishing schedule needs to be worked out. After this tedium, he eats an efficient lunch with an author or an agent, has more staff meetings all afternoon, catches the 7:00 train, arrives home around 8:30, has dinner with his family, and . . .

Do you notice anything missing in this schedule? When does this editor have time to read manuscripts? The answer is, on the train and on weekends. And the manuscripts he's hauling around aren't those dinky 115-page things you see actors-pretending-to-be-editors carry in the movies. Many of them are gut-busting eight-hundred-page monsters. Put yourself in the editor's place. You've got a spouse and three children. You want to spend time with them on the weekend, but you also need to read those manuscripts. You want desperately for those manuscripts to be worth the effort, but you know from experience that most of them will waste your time. How many pages of tediousness will you allow an author before you cram a manuscript back into its box? A hundred pages? Not likely. Fifty pages? Don't make me laugh. *Twenty* pages? Now we're approaching reality. Unless the book is by a proven author, the editor is going to allow the writer twenty pages at best to do something of interest. After that, adios manuscript. All those fabulous touches that the author worked so hard to put into the climax? They're never going to get read if the book doesn't announce that it's worth reading from the start.

Many years ago, I was asked to be a judge for the Mystery Writers of America best-novel Edgar award (so called because Edgar Allan Poe invented the mystery story). I was promised that at most I'd look at about fifty books. But day after day, the UPS driver plodded to my door with his arms full of book boxes that eventually totaled around three hundred. Desperate for a filing system, I arranged laundry baskets throughout the living room, labeling them "new," "awful," "maybe," and "wonderful." Faced with so much to read, I quickly learned how an editor must feel. In fact, the three hundred books littering my living room were nothing compared to the thousands of manuscripts that come to most publishing houses each year. Decisions need to be made in a hurry.

Thus, as one of the Edgar judges, I started by conscientiously reading every book from cover to cover, even if some of them bored me to death. There had to be *something* good in even the worst of them, I thought. But as the deadline approached for submitting my choices and as more books arrived on my doorstep, I stopped reading after fifty pages if a novel hadn't grabbed my attention. By definition, an Edgar-winning book shouldn't be a chore to read, I reminded myself. In a few cases, I tossed a book into the "awful" basket after five pages. On one memorable occasion, this was a novel's first sentence:

He strolled, leisurely, into the park.

I stared at that sentence for a long time. Is there any other way to stroll except leisurely? I asked myself. Why would a writer begin a novel on such a lethargic redundant note? Strolled? And why the commas to emphasize "leisurely"? I turned to page two where a character let out "a blood-curdling scream." At that point, I frisbeed the book into the "awful" basket.

Common sense tells us that the first sentence, the first paragraph, and the first page are where a book makes its strongest impression. Then why would anyone, especially an unknown author desperate to make an impression, begin a book with a page of listless description? Or an ordinary day in the life of the main character? Imagine that you're in a crowd, trying to attract someone's attention. You need to jump higher, wave stronger, and shout louder than everybody else. That doesn't mean you're required to begin with "The shotgun blast blew the groom's head apart, spewing blood and brain all over the white dresses of the flower girls at the wedding." That might be more waving and shouting than an editor would appreciate. As Gene Kelly says in *Singin' in the Rain*, "Dignity, always dignity." But at least, my shotgun example is better than the put-me-to-sleep "He strolled, leisurely, into the park." (Love those commas.)

I recommend that beginning novelists go to a large book store once a month, the kind that has a huge section of novels marked "new releases." Read the first sentence/paragraph/page of every one. Don't pay attention to the type of novel it is. Mystery, romance, thriller, mainstream. Makes no difference. What you're trying to identify is writing that, because of tone or incident or whatever, grabs your attention. You'll be amazed at how many first pages don't manage the job. But we're not interested in those. What we care about are the ones that do grab our attention. Without imitating, use them as examples. Raise your standards. Keep remembering my former editor trying to read manuscripts on the noisy train or on the weekend when he'd much rather be with his family. Above all, pay attention to first sentences. The following are some of my favorites.

> He was an old man who fished alone in a skin in the Gulf Stream and he had gone eighty-four days now without taking a fish.
> —Ernest Hemingway, *The Old Man and the Sea*

> He was born with a gift of laughter and a sense that the world was mad.
> —Rafael Sabatini, *Scaramouche*

> It is a truth universally acknowledged, that a single man in possession of a good fortune must be in want of a wife.
> —Jane Austen, *Pride and Prejudice*

> Many years later, as he faced the firing squad, Colonel Aureliano Buendia was to remember that distant afternoon when his father took him to discover ice.
> —Gabriel Garcia Marquez, *One Hundred Years of Solitude*, trans. Gregory Rabassa

> Last night I dreamt I went to Manderley again.
> —Daphne du Maurier, *Rebecca*

> It was a pleasure to burn.
> —Ray Bradbury, *Fahrenheit 451*

For an extensive list of great first sentences, see Georgianne Ensign's *Great Beginnings*. What they all have in common is a directness that pulls the reader into the narrative, promising a special experience.

First paragraphs ought to have a similar impact. Earlier, I mentioned Geoffrey Household, whose thrillers showed me how that type of fiction could be literary. This is his masterful opening to *Rogue Male*:

I cannot blame them. After all, one doesn't need a telescopic sight to shoot boar and bear; so that when they came on me watching the terrace at a range of 550 yards, it was natural enough that they should jump to conclusions.

What's going on here? I want to know. Why was the narrator watching the house with a rifle and a telescopic sight? Who caught him? What did they do to him? In these few brief sentences, a host of urgent questions controls me.

Here's another great first paragraph. One of the qualities I most admire about it is that the author, knowing his obligation to capture the reader, has created a tone that could just as easily begin a thriller or a horror novel as it does a classic mainstream, socially conscious novel.

As usual, old man Falls had brought John Sartoris into the room with him, had walked the three miles in from the county Poor Farm, fetching, like an odor, like the clean dusty smell of his faded overalls, the spirit of the dead man into that room where the dead man's son sat and where the two of them, pauper and banker, would sit for a half an hour in the company of him who had passed beyond death and then returned.

—William Faulkner, *Sartoris*

I could keep providing examples. Instead, I encourage you to supply your own favorites. Without imitating, use them as your model. Try to write first sentences and paragraphs that create the same tingle that you felt when you first read your own favorite openings. Once you have a distinctive first sentence/paragraph/page, maintain that tone. Keep imagining a very busy, intelligent, experienced editor or agent who would love nothing better than to acknowledge that you've written a masterpiece. The task is, from the start, to get that reader's attention.

In this regard, I try to keep in mind something that Donald E. Westlake once told me. Don is an amazingly versatile productive writer who is perhaps best known for a character named Dortmunder in a series of comic-caper novels, a subgenre that Don invented (*The Hot Rock, Bank Shot*), and who under the name of Richard Stark wrote several intense novels about a professional thief named Parker. I'm one of many writers who admire the Parker books for their economy, directness, and hard-boiled impact. Here are some randomly selected first sentences:

> When a fresh-faced guy in a Chevy offered him a lift, Parker told him to go to hell.
>
> —*Point Blank* (aka *The Hunter)*

> When he didn't get any answer the second time he knocked, Parker kicked the door in.
>
> —*The Split*

> When the knock came at the door, Parker was just turning to the obituary page.
>
> —*The Jugger*

> When the car stopped rolling, Parker kicked out the rest of the windshield and crawled through onto the wrinkled hood.
>
> —*Backflash*

The pattern should be obvious. With a few exceptions in the more-than-twenty Stark/Parker books, all begin with a dynamic "when" clause. Further, every book has the same four-part structure. Sections one, two, and four are from Parker's limited third-person viewpoint. Section three is always from the third-person viewpoint of Parker's antagonist. The series has a remarkable consistency of form. It feels unique.

One evening years ago, at the start of my career, Don advised me to think about writing in the following context. A hundred novels are on a table. Someone has ripped off the covers so that we don't know who wrote the books. The names of famous characters have been changed. There's no explicit indicator to identify who's responsible. Nothing except the writer's tone, his or her approach, the quality of the story and the prose. As we go through these books, Don maintained, we'll soon discover that most of them feel alike, even though each was written by a different person. It's as if a lot of the authors are imitating each other. We put those that feel alike at one end of the table. By the time we finish reading the hundred books, ninety-five are at one end, and five (the distinctive ones) are at the other. Our task, Don said, is to be among those five.

How did I apply this advice to myself? The answer goes back to Stirling Silliphant and *Route 66*. That show was unusual because it combined two elements that we normally don't find together. On the one hand, it was an adventure program whose action could be extreme. In the opening episode, "Black November," for example, a fight came brutally close to a buzz saw. In another episode, "Most Vanquished, Most Victorious," the two main characters fought a Los Angeles street gang, who attacked them with bicycle chains.

But on the other hand, the same episode that featured the buzz saw also had long literate speeches that alluded to *Hamlet* and talked about existential loneliness. The second episode in the series was about a female captain of a shrimp boat in the Gulf of Mexico. Amid plenty of action, the plot was influenced by Shakespeare's *The Taming of the Shrew* and paraphrased a quote from that play as its title, "A Lance of Straw." The third episode, set in New Orleans, evoked the mood of Tennessee Williams. About an outbreak of lethal parrot fever, the script was titled, "The Swan Bed," with overtones of Leda and the Swan as well as the ugly duckling. "The Stone Guest" was about a mining disaster and had numerous allusions to Mozart's *Don Giovanni*. Sartre, Ionesco, and Spinoza were alluded to in other episodes. Frequently, speeches held disguised poetry and went on for several minutes. *One* memorable speech lasted an entire act.

On television, there had never been anything like *Route 66*, and there has never been anything like its combination of action and literacy since then. In retrospect, I realize that the program's preoccupation with philosophers and writers is what made me go to college and eventually get a doctorate in literature. In my teenage letter to Silliphant, I said that I wanted to become him. But as I aged (and as I said many times in these pages), I understood that imitation wasn't the way to go. My goal was to take what I'd learned from Silliphant and make it my own.

Thus I set myself the task of writing thrillers that would appeal to the men and women with whom I'd worked in various factory summer jobs, people with a general education who were grateful for distraction from the tedium of their occupations. The action and suspense in my novels was for them. Simultaneously, I thought of the graduate students and professors I knew at Penn State and the University of Iowa, specialists who weren't satisfied with a book if it didn't feel artistic. My goal was to try to appeal to both sets of readers.

In *Testament*, I peppered the text with allusions to Poe, Melville, Hemingway, Faulkner, just about any American author I admired. I named the main character Reuben Bourne after a character in a Hawthorne story, "Roger Malvin's Burial," which is about guilt and retribution, themes in the novel. I named two policemen Webster and Ford after two well-known seventeenth-century British dramatists, one of whom wrote *The Duchess of Malfi*, a revenge drama (*Testament* is about revenge). I didn't emphasize these allusions. Embedding them so they wouldn't interfere with the narrative, I hoped that they would add a resonance, however.

In *Last Reveille*, I used a historical detail (a bullet stopped a clock during Pancho Villa's historic raid on Columbus, New Mexico) to split time. Thus I started two succeeding chapters with the same sentence: "The rider took the bullet in the neck and toppled." Having marked that point in time, I then led the action in two separate simultaneous directions. I thought of this technique as a sort of cubism on the page. (A troubled reader wrote to tell me, with regret, that the book's printer had repeated a sentence by mistake.)

The Brotherhood of the Rose begins in the middle ages with the story of Eloise and Abelard. *Burnt Sienna* is filled with allusions to Dante and Beatrice. But I bury the literary part of my thrillers so that they're not self-conscious, so that a reader who wants nothing more than thrills won't be distracted. Meanwhile, another kind of reader who needs a literary approach will be pleasantly surprised. This combination is something that I never would have tried if not for Silliphant, and yet the way I do it is different from the poetry that Silliphant employed, not to mention that I'm writing books while he wrote for television and the movies.

Similarly, you need to learn how to adapt the approaches of writers who've inspired you so that you move onward, creating something new. Use your singular background to create themes and approaches unique to you, even though you might have been inspired by other writers. In the end, a first-class you is better than a second-hand version of somebody else. Write books that can't be clumped with a bunch of similar ones. If an editor hasn't seen anything like your writing before, you have a good chance of getting a favorable reading. Of course, some editors are as trendy as some writers and don't see a value in something that isn't part of a current fashion. There's nothing you can do about that. Just keep remembering that first sentence I hated so much. Don't stroll, leisurely, into the park.

The Psychology of Description

Just about every beginning writer knows the agony of the following scenario. You labored hard over a story. You're finally satisfied with it and give it to a friend, spouse, whomever. Fingers crossed, you wait for a response. It never comes soon enough, but when it does, the dialogue is something like this:

Writer: So what do you think?

Reader (squirming): I'm not a professional at this. What do *I* know?

Writer: But you read stories all the time. What's your opinion of *this* one?

Reader (squirming harder): I don't . . . It just didn't . . . It felt kind of . . .

Writer: Felt kind of what?

Reader (gesturing helplessly to find the right word): Thin.

Writer: Thin?

Reader: Yeah. *You* know. Thin.

Writer: No, I *don't* know.

Reader: It felt kind of . . .

Writer: Kind of . . . ?

Reader: Flat.

Writer: Flat?

Reader: One-dimensional.

Writer: You mean the characters?

Reader: No, the characters were interesting. But the whole story just felt . . .

Writer: Yes?

Reader: Thin.

Around and around we go. Thin. Flat. One-dimensional. These words are common reactions, a code of sorts, exasperating to decipher, but here's a clue to their meaning—I once heard a fiction-writing teacher tell his students to imagine that their stories were movies on a television screen above their desks and that all they needed to do was describe what was on the screen. I was horrified.

Why was his advice wrong? Because describing a story as if it were on an imaginary television screen emphasizes the sense of sight. To the degree that your prose is sight-based, it will be flat, thin, and one-dimensional. All on the surface. Like the television. Seems obvious when you think about it. And yet description based solely on sight is a mistake that just about every beginning writer makes. Fortunately, it's also a mistake that's easily corrected.

Earlier, I mentioned John Barth's "Lost in the Funhouse." In that innovative story which is also a kind of essay on fiction writing, Barth notes that, when describing something, it's important "to keep the senses operating." A visual detail should be intersected with one from the other senses, auditory, for instance, so that the reader will be engaged in the scene. "This procedure may be compared to the way surveyors and navigators determine their positions by two or more compass bearings, a process known as triangulation," Barth wrote.

Every time I dramatize a scene, I remind myself of that principle. In fact, seizing on the three parts that are implied in the process of triangulation, I always make a point of crossing a detail of sight with not one but at least two other senses. If I can, I take the sight detail for granted and leave it out.

A good exercise involves deliberately doing without it, as occurs in the following passage from E. M. Forster's *A Passage to India*. A group of people, including a character named Mrs. Moore, enter a cave.

> Crammed with villagers and servants, the circular chamber began to smell. She lost Aziz and Adela in the dark, didn't know who touched her, couldn't breathe, and some vile naked thing struck

her face and settled on her mouth like a pad. She tried to regain the entrance tunnel, but an influx of villagers swept her back. She hit her head. For an instant she went mad, hitting and gasping like a fanatic. For not only did the crush and stench alarm her; there was also a terrifying echo.

Sound, touch, smell, and, by implication, taste (the naked thing on her mouth). Combining these numerous senses creates a multi-dimensional effect. Forster's purpose isn't to make the reader *see* the story. It's to make the reader feel *in* the story. Appealing to several senses goes a long way toward accomplishing that.

Imagine a scene in which a prisoner enters a cell and crosses to his bunk. "He sat on the blanket." Not much going on. Let's enliven it. Should we give the blanket a color? Red? Not in a prison. Blue? Maybe. A faint blue. But I think most readers have already supplied a color. Only one seems appropriate for a prison. Gray. Don't we take that color for granted? Is it even worth mentioning? "He sat on the gray blanket." Still not much going on. Let's apply the triangulation theory. Sound, touch, smell, and taste. Since the prisoner isn't likely to start chewing on the blanket, taste can be eliminated. A detail of smell might be appropriate. "He sat on the blanket. It reeked of sweat." That's palpable. It draws me into the scene. Or how about adding a detail that in one word suggests both sound and touch? "He sat on the scratchy blanket. It reeked of sweat." The scene has become immediate, not thin and flat.

One of the writers most famous for description is Hemingway. (I mention him a lot because my master's thesis was on his style—he's hard-wired into my thoughts.) It's useful to understand how he accomplished his effects. First, his apprenticeship as a reporter for *The Kansas City Star* taught him the value of uncluttered sentences. That newspaper's style sheet emphasized, "Use vigorous English . . . Be positive . . . Avoid the use of adjectives."

But although Hemingway practiced these rules while writing articles, he seems not to have used them in his early fiction, for when he moved to Paris and showed some unpublished stories to

Gertrude Stein, she felt that they were filled with a great deal of "not particularly good description." She told him to throw everything away and start over.

Fate threw it away for him. Months later, while reporting on a peace conference in Switzerland, Hemingway showed some unpublished stories to a fellow journalist, whose reaction was so enthusiastic that Hemingway wrote a letter about it to his first wife, Hadley, in Paris. Excited, she wanted the journalist to see even more of her husband's work, so she packed a suitcase with all of Hemingway's manuscripts: an unfinished novel, eighteen stories, and thirty poems, complete with carbons. At the Paris train station, she bought a ticket to Switzerland and put her luggage in a train compartment. Later she briefly left the compartment. When she came back, she discovered that the suitcase containing the manuscripts had been stolen. Its contents were never recovered.

Hemingway's immediate reaction was to rush to Paris and search his apartment, desperate to believe that only the originals and not the copies also had been put in the suitcase. When he realized that everything in fact was gone, when he thought of the pain that would come with the new start advised by Stein, he was so discouraged that he decided to abandon his dream of becoming a fiction writer. But the urge kept insisting until finally he returned to work, with the difference that this time he went about it in an organized fashion, with the verbal discipline that *The Kansas City Star*'s style sheet recommended.

Hemingway's new organized approach was based on learning basics before he tried to write a novel. He practiced individual sentences, trying to make them as clear and dynamic as possible. To establish viewpoint, he began each with a version of "I have watched" or "I have seen" but took care to emphasize other senses as well. In one, he described a steeplechase race in which the favorite crashed into a barrier and fell kicking while the rest of the horses jumped over it. In another, he described policemen charging a crowd of rioters, beating a kid who looked like a high school football player and who had just shot two of the police officers. See

"One True Sentence" in Carlos Baker's *Ernest Hemingway: A Life Story*. The many details are all in one sentence. Here's an example (Hemingway would later cut back on the adjectives):

> I have watched two Senegalese soldiers in the dim light of the snake house of the Jardin des Plantes teasing the King Cobra who swayed and tightened in tense erect rage as one of the little brown men crouched and feinted at him with his red fez.

Hemingway then moved on to stand-alone dramatic paragraphs (see his collection *In Our Time*). In some, he described incidents of war. Other paragraphs were about bullfighting, a firing squad, and a hanging. All had a vividness that was palpable and prepared him for his next phase: writing short stories. He compared this process to training for longer and longer races until he would eventually go for the marathon of a novel.

Simultaneously, he took writing lessons from Gertrude Stein and from a poet who had recently helped T.S. Eliot edit *The Waste Land* into a masterpiece: Ezra Pound. From these writers, Hemingway learned that less is more, that economy of description can produce clearer effects than descriptions with detail piled upon detail. But economy doesn't only mean reducing a description to its essentials. It also means going for so clean a line that adjectives and adverbs become a sign of bad writing. Pound recommended eliminating them and, only after a long period of abstinence, gradually reintroducing them as an experiment, gauging their effect on a sentence.

Pound's advice remains valid. Adjectives tend to get in the way, overwhelming a description rather than sharpening it. Adverbs tend to have no other function than to strengthen weak verbs ("He went slowly across the room" as opposed to "He shuffled across the room.") and thus encourage wordiness. Or else adverbs can be redundant. Remember "He strolled, leisurely, into the park"? Effective description is in large part dependent on nouns and verbs. Subject, predicate, object. The directness is manifest. Adjective, subject, verb, adverb, adjective, object. The sentence is cluttered.

But Hemingway's vivid description depends on more than just streamlining sentences. It also relies on the power of concrete words. When you read the word "apple," you automatically see an image of that object in your imagination. It's like being hypnotized. Tree—bang, you see one. Waterfall—presto, you're looking at one and probably hearing it. Fire—you feel it. Salt—you taste it. Smoke—you smell it. The process is magical. Concrete words are triggers that instantly prompt you to imagine the physical experience that the words represent.

By comparison, notice how hard it is to deal with abstract words. Honor. What happens in your imagination when you read that word? You see a blank. Your mind struggles. Finally, you associate that abstract word with other abstract words that form some kind of definition like "doing something decently." But what does "decently" mean? Your mind keeps struggling until it comes up with a concrete image of what is supposedly an honorable act. However, that image is likely to be different for various people. In Japan, for example, an honorable act might be using a sword to commit ritual suicide to atone for a shameful act (whatever "shameful" means). Because abstract words have a habit of shifting their meanings, politicians love to use them. What one person thinks "justice" and "morality" mean might not be what the person down the street thinks they mean, and yet many people tend to assume that the politician's meaning of "justice" and "morality" is the same as theirs.

This confusion is the basis for a famous passage in Hemingway's *A Farewell to Arms*. The main character, an ambulance driver in Italy during the First World War, is disgusted by politicians who use words such as "sacred" and "glorious" to prolong the war. The main character has seen nothing glorious, only corpses that remind him of the Chicago stockyards. "Abstract words such as glory, honor, courage, or hallow were obscene beside the concrete names of villages" where battles occurred.

For stylistic and thematic reasons, then, Hemingway relied on concrete words, assembling them in an uncluttered "sequence of motion and fact," as he called it. He avoided adjectives and adverbs because he understood that concrete nouns and verbs are powerful on their own. When he did use adjectives, he tended not to put them immediately next to the nouns they modified but instead to include them later in the sentence, as in this description from *A Farewell to Arms*:

> In the bed of the river there were pebbles and boulders, dry and white in the sun, and the water was clear and swiftly moving and blue in the channels.

Surprisingly, this sentence has five adjectives and one adverb, if you take the time to notice them, but Hemingway usually doesn't give you the time to do that. The sentence is constructed so that the adjectives don't precede the nouns they modify and thus impede the flow of the sentence. Instead, they come after the nouns and stand alone, occupying so strong a place in the sentence that they feel like concrete nouns. The lesson is, when you do need to use adjectives and adverbs, when you can't find any way to avoid them, disguise their use. Don't let the reader catch you at them.

But these suggestions are worthless if your description isn't necessary to begin with. Before the invention of photography, tourists to a fabulous place such as Venice often brought back cheap sketches of St. Mark's piazza that they purchased from local artists. If the travelers were wealthy, they commissioned expensive paintings of the local sights from master artists like Canaletto. Either way, one of the purposes was to let others see what Venice looked like. Later, photographs became a cheaper, quicker way of achieving the same goal. In early novels, description also fulfilled that function. Most readers had no idea what Venice or other exotic places looked like, so novelists supplied pages of description, allowing readers to travel in their imaginations. In the late 1800s, a group of American writers known as local colorists (Sarah Orne Jewett and Hamlin Garland, for example) were popular for their detailed descriptions of remote scenic parts of America. Readers unwilling to brave primitive travel conditions visited attractive back areas vicariously through highly descriptive stories. While there was no doubt beauty in all those felicitous phrases, the primary reason for that abundant description wasn't poetry in prose but, rather, utility. The description was there to provide information.

However, as travel conditions improved, as photography became more widespread and movies came along, this kind of scenic description became unnecessary. Almost everybody these days knows what Venice looks like, even if they haven't been there. A painstaking description of it no longer provides necessary information. Think hard before writing paragraphs and paragraphs of travelogue just because classic writers from previous centuries were required to do so. The rule I follow is that, if I can assume readers are familiar with a place, I don't need to describe it at length. Only if I'm adding something new do I get excited about describing it.

In this regard, I think every writer should spend time listening to tapes of old radio plays (available in many libraries). At their best, radio plays can be amazingly vivid, and yet they rely on almost no description, mostly sound effects and dialogue. The narrator says, "I walked into the skid-row hotel and asked the old guy at the counter for a room." The old guy wheezes and says, "That'll be a buck." We hear four coins being set one at a time on the counter. Then footsteps plod up creaky stairs. Everybody has an idea of what a skid-row hotel looks like. In fact, as soon as you read those words, you saw one in your mind. Its seediness doesn't need to be described. We get the gist through one carefully chosen line of dialogue and a few sounds. When dealing with things that are typical, think of your story as a version of a radio play. You don't need to describe things with which the reader is familiar. Readers will supply obvious details for you, contributing what they take for granted, becoming your coauthor.

Description also fails when it's static. Too often, scenes are constructed so that a character arrives at a locale, the locale is described in one lump, and then the action continues. A much better tactic involves using details of the setting as part of the action. To illustrate, let's describe an ordinary doctor's office. "Marion walked into the doctor's office. It had a chair next to an examination table. There was a glass door on a cabinet through which she saw scalpels and bandages. She sat down and waited nervously." Awful. The two middle sentences are stuck between Marion's walking and sitting. They interrupt. They're static. Your gaze probably slid past them. Also, I'm not crazy about resorting to the adverb "nervously" to tell the reader about Marion's psychological condition. An ordinary doctor's office is just that: ordinary. Why describe it?

I much prefer this alternative: "Marion walked into the doctor's office, sank onto a chair next to the examination table, and stared at the bandages and scalpels behind the glass door of a cabinet." Basically, I've combined narrative with description, disguising the description so that it's part of the action. This stealth description is effective because it accomplishes two functions at once, simultaneously establishing the setting and dramatizing Marion's attitude toward it. Why do the bandages and the scalpel make her stare? Without explicitly stating it, the sentence implies that Marion is nervous.

What about describing a character's body? The most unusual physical description I know comes at the start of Dashiell Hammett's *The Maltese Falcon*.

> Samuel Spade's jaw was long and bony, his chin a jutting V under the more flexible V of his mouth. His nostrils curved back to make another, smaller, V. His yellow-grey eyes were horizontal. The V motif was picked up again by thickish brows rising outward from twin creases above a hooked nose, and his pale brown hair grew down—from high flat temples—in a point on his forehead.

If you get a pencil and use Vs to sketch a simplified version of Hammett's description, you see the following:

As Hammett says at the end of the paragraph, Spade looked rather pleasantly "like a blond satan."

But this is an amusing trick, a limited device that I don't recommend you try unless you find an unself-conscious variation on it. It won't help you establish a consistent approach to describing people. In *The End of the Affair*, Graham Greene has his first-person narrator (a novelist) write the following in response to seeing his former lover:

> How can I make a stranger see her as she stopped in the hall at the foot of the stairs and turned to us? I have never been able to describe even my fictitious characters except by their actions. It has always seemed to me that in a novel the reader should be allowed to imagine a character in any way he chooses.

Exactly. As a reader, I dislike it when an author gives me a lengthy physical description of a character. I need to pause to visualize the specifics that the author is foisting upon me. Often I find them confusing. I would much rather have the freedom to imagine what the character looks like, and I apply this principle when I think of my own readers. With Greene, I believe that readers can do a lot more efficient job of imagining the look of characters than *I* can and that characters are best described by their actions.

Introducing a character, giving a sense of that character's physique is one of the most challenging tasks a writer faces. A character walks into a room. Is she short, tall, or of medium height? Is she fair or dark? What about her hair: blond, brunette, redheaded, streaked? Long hair? Short? Curly? Is she attractive or ordinary-looking? Is she thin or heavy? Big-busted or small? What's she wearing? Evening clothes? Jeans? Rags? A business suit?

These choices can drive an author crazy. Unless a character's choice of clothing, footwear, hair style, and jewelry implies something about his or her personality, it doesn't make much difference if somebody wears jeans as opposed to shorts or a T-shirt as opposed to a denim shirt with the sleeves rolled up. John Barth calls these latter details fill-in-the-blank writing and sometimes humorously declines to provide those details, inviting the reader to do the job for him: "The brown hair on Ambrose's mother's fore-arms gleamed in the sun like." As the abrupt end of that sentence from "Lost in the Funhouse" indicates, there's a blank space—something must fill it, but perhaps one detail would be as good as another. Keep that aspect of the description brief and emphasize the effect that a character's appearance has on others. Does the character radiate power or sexuality? Does the character's posture suggest insecurity? Do her eyes communicate fear? Do her clothes suggest vanity? The objective details of a character's appearance don't matter as much as the emotions they imply. If you concen-trate on a character's emotional effect, the reader will supply the physical details. "Her eyes were the key—and the captivating spirit behind them." The reader does the rest of the work.

When describing the title character of *Anna Karenina*, Tolstoy prefers brief, impressionistic passages rather than elaborate, detailed ones. Often the purpose of the description is to show how other characters react to her. Instead of a full-blown depiction of her gestures and facial expressions, their overall quality is emphasized, as seen from another character's perspective. Here's an example:

> Her brilliant grey eyes, shadowed by thick lashes, gave [Vronsky] a friendly, attentive look, as though she were recognizing him, and then turned to the approaching crowd as if in search of someone. In that brief glance Vronsky had time to notice the suppressed anima-tion which played over her face and flitted between her sparkling

eyes and the slight smile curving her red lips. It was as though her nature were so brimming over with something that against her will it expressed itself now in a radiant look, now in a smile.

—translated by Rosemary Edmonds

Note the combination of the specific ("brilliant grey eyes" and "thick lashes") with the general ("friendly, attentive"). The latter is a version of fiction-as-a-radio-play. Anna looked "friendly." The reader supplies the specifics of what it means to look friendly. (This is also a favorite Hemingway device. "The town was pleasant.") Note, too, that Tolstoy concludes with the general impression Anna creates—that she's so full of life that it brims over into her smiles.

Keep asking yourself, "What does the reader absolutely need to be aware of at this moment in the story?" If you provide no more and no less information than you sense the reader requires, if you make your description uncluttered, based on concrete words and an appeal to many senses (in the Tolstoy example, "brilliant," "sparkling," and "radiant" fulfill the "touch" requirement, describing the way light hits the spectator's eyes), if you serve the requirements of your story and not the conventions of novels from a pre-photography culture, you're on your way to writing effective description.

What Not To Do in Dialogue

How to create first-rate dialogue isn't something that can be taught, but it's easy to learn how to avoid the common mistakes that lead to dialogue that isn't acceptable. So many errors come to mind that I'm going to choose one arbitrarily: the use of names.

> "Jill, I'm going downtown to the library," Jack said.
> "Okay, Jack, I'll see you later," Jill said.

The needlessness of the repetition should be obvious, and yet I see writers repeating names all the time. Because the speech tags indicate which character is speaking, it isn't necessary, within the dialogue, to include the name of the person being addressed. Perhaps someone might object that names need to be included in dialogue for the sake of verisimilitude, to imitate the way we speak in life. The problem is that, for the most part, we do not in fact speak this way. Try an experiment. Listen to conversations with no other purpose than that of noting how often people say each other's names. It seldom happens, and when it does, it feels unusual.

As near as I can guess, many writers throw names into dialogue whenever they can because they're not imitating dialogue in life; they're imitating dialogue in the movies. On the screen, names need to be said often—at least a couple of times in each scene— in order to identify the characters. But fiction writing isn't movie writing. As a discipline, to unlearn the unfortunate habits the movies have taught us, I recommend eliminating names from dialogue completely. When this avoidance becomes second nature, slowly introduce names in dialogue but only when absolutely necessary. You'll find that it feels right to use names in dialogue when those names are included for unavoidable reasons—when people are being introduced to each other, when people are identifying themselves at the start of a telephone conversation or during a dark scene in a cellar, in short when there is no other way for a character to find out the identity of the person to whom that character is speaking. Or when there is no other way for *the reader* to find out a name.

Let's go back to the initial example. This time, the dialogue and the use of names within it are more acceptable.

> "Jill, I'm going downtown to the library."
> "Okay, Jack, I'll see you later."

This exchange isn't exactly true to life. I'm still not sure that Jack and Jill would go to the trouble of addressing each other. They know who they are, after all. Better to eliminate the names completely and use another identifying device. But because the clumsiness and wordiness of the initial example have been eliminated, the dialogue at least doesn't draw attention to itself. What has made the difference, of course, is that the speech tags have been cut out. Not a bad idea, it seems to me, for speech tags are an especially troublesome device, as you'll see in the following example.

> "I'll track you down and murder you!" Jill hissed.

Apparently Jack failed to return from the library. Big mistake. So is the one in the dialogue, which should be obvious. You can't hiss if you don't use sibilants, and there aren't any in this speech. How about "Jill growled"? It won't work. In this speech, only "down" has the lower-register sound that we associate with a growl. "Jill spat"? Have you ever seen anyone spit words? And anyway, "spat" doesn't really communicate the sense of what the writer is trying to say. Similarly, characters shouldn't bark, rasp, or rumble their dialogue. At best, these expressions are inaccurate. At worst, they're cliches or even unintentional parodies as in "'Keep away from the bomb!' he exploded." In either case, they draw attention to themselves, and as was the case when names were used within dialogue, drawing unwanted attention is exactly what you don't want to do.

To eliminate the problem, restrict the verbs used in speech tags to "said" and "asked." In extreme cases, "demanded" or "insisted" may be used, and "shouted" or "screamed"—although isn't that why exclamation marks were invented, to indicate that someone is shouting or screaming? But let's include the latter two anyhow. And maybe "whispered" or "murmured." Not many. If you limit your speech tags accordingly, you'll discover some interesting consequences. One is that your tone will be less likely to be melodramatic. Another is that any weakness in your dialogue will become more obvious once the crutch of an overwritten speech tag has been eliminated. Yet another benefit is that you'll start to question the need for any speech tags at all.

Let's look at speech tags more closely.

"I'll track you down and murder you!" Jill said.

After the exclamation mark, "said" seems an understatement.

"I'll track you down and murder you!" Jill shouted.

"Shouted" is redundant. So what is the proper verb? Do we surrender and say that speech tags are inherently problematic, a necessary evil? Or do we look for a better way? After all, what is the purpose for a speech tag? Only one—to identify the speaker. But suppose what comes after Jill isn't a verb of speech. Why can't it be one of action or description?

"I'll track you down and murder you!" Jill's cheeks were as scarlet as her hair.

Now that added sentence isn't going to win anyone a Pulitzer prize, but on the basis of economy, it does a good job. First, it provides a dramatization of Jill's anger (without the triteness of actually using the word "anger"). Second, it adds a physical detail that makes Jill more vivid to us.

That last point deserves elaboration. Unfortunately, description is almost always used in uneventful moments, when someone strolls into a room, for example. We feel description coming on, and we go to sleep. Why not include description a little at a time— where there would normally be fill-in-the-blank speech tags?

"I'll stab you in your sleep." Jill's eyes meant every word.

The "Jill said" has been eliminated, but we don't miss it. We know who the speaker is. We intuit how the dialogue was said. There aren't any empty words. Of course, you can change the passage and decide that you want another detail besides Jill's eyes. But as the passage now stands, on its own terms, it has reached a useful reduction. I especially like the notion that Jill's eyes aren't described—the reader does the work for the writer.

I don't want to give the impression that I'm against speech tags entirely. When carefully placed, their fill-in-the-blank quality can create interesting effects—subtle pauses, for example.

"I know he doesn't believe I'll come after him," Jill said. "His mistake."

Take out "Jill said," and the progression of the dialogue isn't as dramatic. Sometimes "Jill said" can be a version of "Jill hesitated" or "Jill thought about it." Conversely, "Jill hesitated" is sometimes more effective than "Jill said." Every speech tag is a challenge. Sometimes, for variety, writers invert a speech tag: "said Jill." I do not recommend this approach. It is not idiomatic and distracts the reader from what is being said.

While we consider speech tags, the topic of adverbs can't be ignored.

"I gave that jerk the best three days of my life," Jill said bitterly.

It shouldn't be a surprise that "bitterly" is redundant, and yet we often come across redundancy of this sort. Does the speech tag look so lonely with its meager function of identification that some writers can't resist giving the verb a companion? The temptation needs to be resisted. If the dialogue communicates what it is supposed to, the adverb in the speech tag isn't necessary, and if the dialogue fails to communicate what it is supposed to, the adverb merely points out that the dialogue hasn't been successful.

One of the few cases in which a speech tag's adverb would be acceptable involves dialogue that is meant to be spoken in contradiction to its apparent sense.

"I gave that jerk the best three days of my life," Jill said proudly.

Here the adverb contributes something. The better way, though, would have been to cut "Jill said proudly" and add a narrative sentence in which Jill does something in a proud manner (but without the use of the word "proud").

"I gave that jerk the best three days of my life." Jill shoved back her shoulders and stood straighter.

Remember the advice Gertrude Stein and Ezra Pound gave Hemingway about adverbs? Eliminate them entirely until you learn to use them judiciously. If that advice was good enough for Hemingway . . .

And then there are the problems associated with punctuation in dialogue, specifically the exclamation mark. Horror and thriller writers are especially inclined to overuse it. Page for page, there are more exclamation marks in horror and thriller dialogue than in any other type of narrative. Do some horror and thriller writers believe that by adding a lot of exclamation marks when characters verbally react to terrifying situations, the situations are going to be even more terrifying than they would be with a plain old simple period? If so, they are wrong. By its nature, the exclamation mark is an attention-getting device. It upstages. It draws attention to itself. When overused, it can even push the reader away, distancing rather than engaging.

To get in the habit of not overusing the exclamation mark . . . well, by now, you probably anticipated my recommendation. Don't use exclamation marks at all. After several hundred pages of purity, you can then slowly reintroduce them, one at a time, in special situations, after soul-searching justification. Some of you might object that it's impossible to avoid exclamation marks. I disagree. Note the following:

"You son of a bitch, I hate your guts!" Jill shouted.

Poor Jill has finally found Jack, but she still has her problems, and so does her dialogue. The speech tag is redundant. So is the exclamation mark, which is implied by "You son of a bitch." The whole business feels stagy, hysterical, and off-putting. But let's try it this way:

"You son of a bitch, I hate your guts." Jill's gaze never left his.

The intensity has been retained, but the staginess is now eliminated. By cutting the speech tag and exclamation mark, the writer found a better way to present the dialogue.

No one is going to complain that "Look out, she's got a knife!" involves an unnecessary use of the exclamation mark, but suppose "My God" is substituted for "Look out." "My God, she's got a knife!" is a much stronger statement, perhaps too strong if you've got fifteen exclamation marks on the same page. "My God" implies an exclamation. It probably doesn't need enhancement. "My God, she's got a knife." I don't miss the exclamation mark. This sort of bartering should become a deliberate exercise. Add and subtract to avoid stabbing the reader in the eye with too many !!!!.

Another punctuation problem that intrigues me is how to add

emphasis to a question.

"What am I going to do?" Jill exclaimed.

Well, for starters, Jill, you should stop exclaiming. But "shouted" doesn't do the job, nor does "shrieked." "Wailed"? Maybe, but it's still melodramatic. Using an exclamation mark after a question mark as in "What am I going to do?!" is an abomination. Let's try this:

Jill could barely get the words out. "What am I going to do?"

Again, finding a substitute for a speech tag led to a solution.

"*What am I going to do?*" Jill stared at everybody in the library.

Here, the italics serve the same function as an exclamation mark. When used in moderation, they are an acceptable way to enliven questions and sometimes to improve the drab look of a page. But remember, if the question has some form of cursing, the italics become redundant just as an exclamation mark is redundant after a statement that contains cursing.

If the passage absolutely demands cursing, be moderate. A little of it goes a long way. I've seen beginning writers pepper curse words through sentence after sentence.

"If you don't blanking get your blank blank into this blank house this blanking minute, I'm going to blank your blank and nail it to the blanking door."

Two things happen when I read this junk. I get bored, and I get angry. I didn't pick up your book to read garbage. If this is as clever as you can be, I don't want to read your prose. In life, if you met somebody who spoke this way, you'd want to flee. Then why put this stuff on the page? As near as I can determine, this abomination occurs because a writer is corrupted by the awful blanking dialogue that movies inflict on us these days. It's also a sign of insecurity. The writer wonders if the dialogue is strong enough and decides that a lot of blanking blanks will do the trick. Someone might object that this kind of dialogue is realistic in certain situations, in tense scenes involving policemen or soldiers, for example. I can only reply that in my research I spend considerable time with policemen and soldiers. Few of them curse any more than a normal person would. This garbage isn't realistic. It merely draws attention to itself and holds back the story. Use it sparingly.

A further category: colloquialisms. A certain amount of "well," "yeah," "you know," "okay," and the like are necessary to create the illusion of verisimilitude, but unless Jill is a Valley Girl and vapid expressions are a method of characterizing her, this sort of filler should be used in moderation. The words don't say anything, after all. They are blank spots on the page and impede the flow of the story. Slang, too, is a form of colloquialism. It's necessary to enliven dialogue, but unfortunately slang quickly becomes dated.

"That's cool. Give me a high five."

At one time, those expressions were fresh. A novelist who used them when they were current would have seemed "with it, in the groove." Those same expressions are now embarrassing, and that novelist's once fresh-seeming book is now dated. Unless your character is a parody, there's no reason to inflict trite, soon to be old-fashioned expressions on both your character and your reader. To avoid the problem, invent your own slang.

What about spelling words the way someone sloppy with diction would pronounce them?

"Dinja know he wuz gonna gitcha?"

I've never been fond of the technique because it upstages the dialogue. One of the few novelists I think handles it well is Mark Twain in *Adventures of Huckleberry Finn*. Before the advent of phono-

graph records and coast-to-coast radio, Twain's depictions of
various American dialects had an instructional value. Not many
Americans would have heard the distinctive ways people along the
Mississippi spoke. Reading the dialects would have been an education, whereas now we're so used to hearing Southern accents in
movies and on television that they're cliches. Even Twain had his
doubts about spelling words according to their sounds, prefacing
his novel with an assurance to the reader that he had tried hard to
be true to the various dialects. "I make this explanation," he wrote,
"for the reason that without it many readers would suppose that
all these characters were trying to talk alike and not succeeding."

My immediate response to "Dinja know he wuz gonna
gitcha?" is to note the unusual spelling. Struck by the self-
conscious dialogue, I slow my reading to try to understand what
the character is actually saying. By then, the impetus of the
narrative has been stalled. Sometimes, of course, a character is so
illiterate that unusual spelling needs to be employed. But must
there be so much of it?

"Didn't you know he was gonna get you?"

For my taste, the single misspelling adequately dramatizes the character's illiteracy without the expense of obstructing the narrative.

Don't let yourself be contaminated by dialogue from the
movies, the radio, or the stage, that is, dialogue spoken out loud.
Years ago, when I was a professor, I had a graduate student who'd
been a news announcer. He was assigned to read a report to the
class and did it brilliantly, his voice getting every nuance out of
every word. But my suspicions were aroused, and when I asked to
see the text of the report, I wasn't surprised to find that on the
page the text was flat and cliched. The student had been relying
on a tone that he imposed. "I've discovered how to write
dialogue," someone once told me. "I talk into a tape recorder and
pretend I'm various characters speaking to one another. Then I
transcribe the results." A variation is to read dialogue out loud
after it's written, to see how natural it sounds. All are bad ideas.

They tempt a writer to add inflection, to supply a tone and a drive that are perhaps not in fact on the page. One of the few reasons to read dialogue out loud is to verify a suspicion that it's awkward or phony. In fiction, dialogue is an act of silent communication. You can't rely on a reader to imagine that your characters speak with the inflection you intend. Rather, you need to invent visual cues that will force the reader to imagine the tone you require.

Telephone conversations require speech tags emphasizing that the characters are not face-to-face. Consider the following:

> Jill picked up the phone. "Hello?"
> "Hi, this is Jack."
> "Where are you? I've been looking everywhere."
> "I'm at the airport," Jack said.
> "The airport? What are you doing there?" Jill asked.
> "I'm leaving you," Jack said.
> "Well, you'd better go far, because I'm coming after you." Jill slammed down the phone.

Except for the first and last sentences of this sequence, you'd never know this was a phone conversation. The distance between the characters isn't emphasized. A better version would be as follows:

> Jill picked up the phone. "Hello."
> "Hi, this is Jack." The familiar voice sounded distant.
> "Where are you? I've been looking everywhere."
> "I'm at the airport." Jack's tone wavered, as if he were nervous.
> "The airport?" Jill clutched the phone so hard that her fingers cramped. "What are you doing there?"
> "I'm leaving you." Jack sounded relieved to have said it.
> "Well, you'd better go far, because I'm coming after you." Jill slammed down the phone.

It seems obvious that a telephone conversation requires references to sounds, voices, and the feel of the phone, and yet many writers fail to include them. This error is more widespread now that cell phones are commonplace in novels.

Which authors impress me with their dialogue? George V. Higgins (*The Friends of Eddie Coyle*) and Elmore Leonard (*Get Shorty*) come immediately to mind—because they invent their own vivid slang and use engaging colloquial rhythm. I'm also impressed by Hemingway's lean approach in "A Clean Well-Lighted Place" and James M. Cain's in *The Postman Always Rings Twice*. For each of these latter two writers, every word of dialogue is carefully considered and never wasted. The more I read them, the more I learn from them. Here's a passage from Cain:

> "Frank."
> "Yes?"
> "He's coming home tomorrow. You know what that means?"
> "I know."
> "I got to sleep with him, 'stead of you."
> "You would, except that when he gets here we're going to be gone."
> "I was hoping you'd say that."
> "Just you and me and the road, Cora."
> "Just you and me and the road."
> "Just a couple of tramps."
> "Just a couple of gypsies, but we'll be together."
> "That's it. We'll be together."

Note how vivid this dialogue looks on the page, how easily the eyes glide down it. There aren't any speech tags. Cain avoids them whenever possible. He mentions the characters' names, Frank and Cora, once each in this exchange. Earlier, I said that I'm uncomfortable when names are used in dialogue, but here, I don't see how the device can be avoided, given the absence of speech tags. Moreover, this intimate context is one of the few examples in which the inclusion of names feels somewhat natural. The line "I got to sleep with him, 'stead of you" is the only example of illiteracy in the exchange and is sufficient to characterize these people. Any further use of illiteracy would be tedious.

When you read these experts in dialogue and try to learn from them, be careful as always not to imitate. Your task is to be inspired by them to find your own way. But ultimately, no matter how much you avoid the technical problems I discussed, there is only one method of creating effective dialogue, and that is by concentrating on the essence of dialogue, by doing the hardest thing of all and giving your characters something interesting to say.

Dealing with Writer's Block

Writer's block refers to a terrifying stasis in which a writer accustomed to a regular output suddenly finds that the words aren't coming any longer, that the mind is blank and the creative well has seemingly gone dry. This can go on for a day, a week, a month . . . I've heard of a few writers who agonized with it for years. Conversely, some writers claim never to have experienced it. Everybody's different. The two major blocks I suffered had different causes: a problem with my psyche and a problem with what I was writing. One of these is the usual culprit. The trick is to identify what needs to be fixed—the writer or what's being written.

My first major block occurred during the composition of my second novel, *Testament*. For a year, I couldn't put two words together. Looking back over the decades, I now understand what my trouble was. I had somehow managed to complete my first novel, *First Blood*. My publisher wanted a second one sooner rather than later. Feeling pressured, I kept thinking of the good reviews that *First Blood* received and worrying that the critics wouldn't like my second effort. I kept comparing the second novel to the first and getting nervous because they were different. I started competing with myself, becoming so self-conscious that the second novel couldn't command my mind's attention.

This particular instance of writer's block is sometimes called the Second Novel Syndrome (a serious condition—many first novelists never write a second). But painful self-consciousness can occur at any time. Doubt is part of the baggage most writers carry. Even those with amazingly long successful careers sometimes wonder if yesterday's pages will make them throw up. I finally broke the block by forgetting about me (whom I'd started to dislike) and concentrating on the story. Easier said than done.

On a practical basis, I found that if I didn't strive for perfection, if I just somehow got through the wretched scene I was struggling with, the next scene became a little easier. I realized that I could always go back and fix an awkward scene but that I couldn't fix anything if I hadn't written it. Motion became my purpose. I gave myself permission to make mistakes, reassuring myself that, when the book was finished, everything would be made right.

A writer friend once spent a month rewriting the same page. A transition in the middle kept giving him trouble and throwing off the scene's rhythm, so he reworked that page and reworked it, trying to make it the most perfect page ever. To me, it was obvious that he was too close to the problem, that he'd become over-scrupulous. I told him, "Forget that page. Come back to it later." But he was determined to fix it now. "Now" turned out to last a long time, and he never did like that page, even when the book was published. But to me, that page seemed fine. The problem wasn't with the page. The problem was in my friend's mind.

How to avoid this? Over the years, I've learned to keep watch for this evil twin part of my personality. When I start to fixate on a problem in one project, I switch to another and quite different project. Sometimes I switch from fiction to non-fiction and vice versa. I have a file of short story ideas that I turn to if I get stuck in a novel. If short fiction doesn't appeal to you, write book reviews for your local newspaper. Write an essay. Start a letter to yourself about another project. Write *something*. Motion and change. Those are the solutions when the problem is in your head.

But sometimes the problem is in fact on the page. As I mentioned, characters in a story will occasionally refuse to do what you want them to. The plot will freeze because of illogic and faulty motivation. Don't panic. Don't tell yourself that you've lost your talent and you're all washed up. Stop thinking about yourself and concentrate on eliminating possible plot and character causes for the block.

That's what I did the second time I suffered a major block. The event occurred twenty years after *Testament*. It involved my thirteenth novel, *Extreme Denial*. With so much experience, you'd think I'd know what I was doing, but every book is a new adventure. Again proving how humble I am, I'll expose my mistakes. The idea for that novel came from a Martin Scorsese gangster movie, *Goodfellas*, that concluded with a thug being admitted to the government's Witness Relocation program. I thought, "Wouldn't it be awful to live next door to a monster like that, to become friends with him and not realize how evil and dangerous he was until former buddies of his showed up to try to silence him."

An ever-alert part of my imagination said, "Pay attention, David. That sounds like the basis for a novel." So I wrote my conversation with myself (too hastily, it turned out) and then produced one hundred and fifty pages of manuscript before the novel froze.

"Damn, I've got another block," I told myself. "I'm a rotten writer. I always was." Blah, blah, blah.

Here's the plot as I'd conceived it. Our hero, Steve, is an intelligence officer who left the CIA because he couldn't stand the way bureaucratic mistakes can cost operatives their lives. In a way, he's a modern version of a retired gunslinger. Steve has a wife and a son and works as a real-estate agent. Basic, normal, kind of boring life. His next-door buddy, Ray, sells insurance. He's a pillar of the community, coaches Little League, etc. In fact, Steve's son belongs to Little League, and one afternoon, when Steve is at a game, helping Ray, enjoying quality family time, gangsters start shooting at Ray. Steve's son is wounded. Ray escapes and disappears. During the investigation, Steve learns that Ray used to be an enforcer for the mob, that Ray was lying to the community and using Steve's family as part of his cover. Furious about being betrayed by a man he thought was his best friend, Steve steps back into his former life, determined to track down Ray and get even.

That's where the book froze. You probably see the trouble, but I was too close to the project to know what was wrong. Somebody next door turns out to be not what that person seems. Our hero feels betrayed and wants to get even. Those are the plot's essentials. So why couldn't I move the book forward? A day went by. A week. Finally, in desperation, I phoned my editor and told him that I didn't think I'd be able to deliver the book on schedule. The plot was seriously flawed. Never should have tried it. Blah, blah. After the editor calmed me down, which is another talent good editors have, he suggested a metaphoric version of dynamite to blow apart the block.

"Change your characters' sexes. Do something drastic to see the plot in a new way and expose the problem."

Change the characters' sexes? I thought. Why, that's the dumbest idea I ever heard.

So I thanked my editor for his advice and ended the phone call. Change the characters' sexes? Ridiculous. Look what happens if I make the guy next door a woman. The plot won't work anymore. It . . .

Wham! I suddenly realized my mistake. A former mob enforcer lives next door to our hero, but our hero thinks he's a friend. Our hero's son gets wounded because of hit men trying to keep the enforcer from testifying. The boy's in the hospital. Mom's scared to death. And what does my hero do? He goes after his former friend. Nonsense. What any believable person (at least any person I care to read about) would do is stay with his family and make sure they're safe. With the best intentions, I'd created an idiot plot. The reason the plot wouldn't move forward is that my hero wouldn't let me write the scene in which he told his wife and son, "Good luck. I'll see you later. Son, get well soon. I'm off to settle a score." There isn't any way to write that scene. It has no human truth. Trapped by the plot, I had blamed my meager abilities for failing to move events forward. Instead, I should have tried to find a nuts-and-bolts reason for the plot's stasis. Often, the problem is a wrong viewpoint. But in this case, the characters were ill-conceived.

I went back to my written conversation and continued where it had ended.

"Good morning, David. How are you today?"

"Awful. Miserable."

"What's the problem?"

"I created an idiot plot. The book won't work if the hero has a family."

"Then take the family out."

"Which leaves me with a bad guy and a good guy living next door to each other. The good guy gets mad when he realizes that the bad guy isn't what he seems. The good guy decides to track him down. But that doesn't make sense. If the good guy doesn't have a son who gets shot because of the bad guy, the good guy doesn't have a strong reason to want to get even."

"Maybe the bad guy causes the hero's sister to get shot."

"Which basically means I need to create a character just so she can get hurt. The same with the hero's son. I never liked the little brat. The plot forced me to put him in the book."

"David, it sounds as if you don't yet have the right angle on the material."

"No kidding. My editor says I should make the guy next door a woman."

"And what will that accomplish?"

"How should *I* know? The woman's in the Witness Relocation program, right? The same situation as before. And my hero thinks she's an upstanding citizen, the same as before. What do I gain by changing the sex of the character? What's the benefit of . . . Wait. Suppose he falls in love with her? Her house blows up. She disappears. Neighbors say they saw her running out the back of her property and getting in a man's car. Investigators admit to my hero that they put her in the house next door because they thought she'd be safer if she lived close to a former intelligence officer. It looks like she's only been pretending to love him. A situation like that could definitely make my hero feel angry. He goes after her, to rescue her and make her look him in the eyes and answer the question, 'Did you love me, or were you using me?'"

Suddenly character and not situation controlled the plot. Excited by the book's fresh direction, I began anew and wrote

Extreme Denial quickly once I realized my mistakes. But I couldn't have done it without considering my editor's suggestion that I try a different perspective and then using my written conversation with myself to analyze the implications. If you don't have the benefit of an editor, you still have your written conversation in which you can argue with yourself and question the assumptions upon which the plot is based. Sometimes, the one thing you believe is absolutely essential to the plot is the one thing that needs to be changed. Take nothing for granted.

Or maybe you're just in need of a rest. Or maybe you truly need a shrink. But before you spend money for psychological counseling, buy Dennis Palumbo's *Writing from the Inside Out: Transforming Your Psychological Blocks to Release the Writer Within*. Palumbo used to be a television and movie writer (*Welcome Back, Kotter; My Favorite Year*). He then became a therapist who specializes in helping writers overcome psychological problems, and Lord knows writers have a lot of such problems. Otherwise we wouldn't be writers. In an entertaining, productive way, Palumbo addresses just about every fiction writer's psychological problem I can imagine. Keep it on your bedside table. Refer to it often, and remember: motion, motion, motion.

A couple of methods that cure writer's block come from Neuro-Linguistic Programming. NLP is a way of using language to solve personal problems and to integrate our thoughts and emotions in a constructive manner. I first heard about it when an intelligence operative I was interviewing mentioned that many intelligence agencies teach NLP to their personnel as an aid to recruiting and debriefing informants. Always happy to do research, I learned so much about it that I became a certified practitioner. Here is a simplified application of NLP to the problem of writer's block.

NLP maintains that many of our dilemmas occur because we are either too associated or too disassociated with something. That "something" often involves either the past or the future. The following graph is a useful way to visualize these polarities.

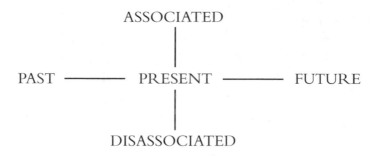

Ideally, what you want is for everything to be balanced in the center—in the present. How do you accomplish that? First, you need to identify the problem. Look at the graph. Examine each section. Decide which combination applies to you. Perhaps, like me when I was blocked during the composition of *Testament*, you can't move a project forward because you're fixated on what you wrote in the past.

To break from the past, remind yourself of the most creative session you had when you wrote the prose you think is better. Recall where you were sitting, the time of day, the season, what the light was like. Imagine the joy of composition that you experienced. Make it as vivid as possible. Press a hand on one of your shoulders (or the back of an elbow or some other slightly-out-of-the-way spot). Get up. Leave the room. Read a page in a magazine. Come back. Sit down. Imagine how pleased you're going to be when your current project is completed. How thrilled you'll be to type "The End." How exciting it'll be to submit the manuscript. Press your shoulder again. Remember the joy of creating that you experienced a few minutes earlier. Start composing. Now. Right here. In the present.

In effect, you're hypnotizing yourself. Using positive commands, you have isolated a useful emotion from your otherwise unhealthy preoccupation with the past. The first time you pressed your shoulder, you established an association with that body part and the creative feelings that you're taking from the past and applying to the present. Getting up, leaving the room, reading a page in a magazine, and coming back were what NLP calls a "break state," a way to give your mind and emotions a brief rest. When you

pressed your shoulder the second time, simultaneously concentrating on how good it feels to be creative, you made the transfer,
disassociating from the past and associating with the present to
accomplish something in the future. On later occasions, without
overdoing it, touch your shoulder, simultaneously concentrating
on that creative emotion, when you have trouble putting yourself
in a mood to write.

A while ago, I mentioned a writer who had so associated with
a page in his manuscript that he was constantly rewriting it instead
of moving on. To disassociate from the problem, two things are
necessary. First, you need a break state, which you produce by
telling yourself forcefully that the page is good enough for now.
Simultaneously close your eyes. Imagine the page in your mind.
It'll be big. Make it smaller. Even smaller. So small that you're
viewing the page through the reverse end of a telescope. The page
is the size of a postage stamp. The page has vanished. Without
opening your eyes, turn the page on your desk, or if you're using
a computer, look down at the keyboard and scroll forward until,
when you look up, you're facing a blank. Touch your left shoulder.
Remember the intense creative feeling you've learned to rely on.
Write. Keep writing. You hypnotized yourself into dissociating
from the problematic page and associating with the next one. In
this context, you might also want to associate with the future by
realizing how thrilled you will be at the end of the session when
you will have accomplished something new.

All writers can benefit from learning about Neuro-Linguistic
Programming. Read a basic introduction to it, preferably one that
has a section on creativity, although taking a course or having a
session with a practitioner would make NLP's theories more vivid.
Among other things, you'll discover which sensory orientation you
prefer. Most people tend to be either visual, auditory, or kinesthetic,
with room for combinations. I'm primarily a "touch" person, with
a secondary reliance on sight. Thus a lot of the details in my books
are based on touch and feeling. If you're primarily a "sight" person,
the chances are that you employ a lot of details based on seeing, in

which case you need to be on guard because, as you know from the lesson on description, "sight" details are the weakest.

In terms of eliminating writer's block, the following are the two easiest NLP ways to do it. Ask for help from the writer you most admire. But don't ask that writer in person. Imagine that the writer is in the room with you, looking over your shoulder. Feel that person filling the space behind you. In my case, I imagine Philip Klass. I say, "Phil, I'm stuck. I've been working on this section for three weeks, and the only results are my chewed finger-nails. What would *you* do? Tell me how to get moving." If you make the transfer powerfully enough, you'll get an answer. It might not be the answer you expect, but it *will* be an answer. For instance, the imagined writer might say to you, "What's the big deal? The story's fine. You're just too close to it. You need a rest." Or the imagined writer might say, "You're right. The story's lost its way. Let's reexamine some of your assumptions about it." Or the imagined writer might say, "Remember, I solved a problem like this in [name your favorite book]." Now you've added a second NLP exercise, accessing your idol's creativity.

These positive self-manipulations can be fun. Here's my favorite. Somebody's in a terrible state about his or her writing, has an absolutely insoluble problem, can't move forward, and is ready to jump in a lake.

You: So the problem's absolutely insoluble?
Other: Absolutely. Can't be solved. Worst problem anybody ever had. Totally baffling.
You: Can't be solved?
Other: Impossible.
You: Well, if you did know how to solve it, what would the answer be?
Other: If I did know how to solve it?
You: Yes. If you did know how to solve it.
Other: Oh, in that case, if I did know how to solve it, the answer would be . . .

With the power of that "if" clause, the stuck writer will solve the writing problem. But obviously, we're not talking about somebody else. We're talking about you. Go through that dialogue with yourself. If you did know the answer, what would it be? Again, the answer you inevitably get might not be the one you expect, but it *will* be an answer, and it will be helpful. Note that this exercise is useful when it comes to other kinds of problems, also. Learning how to solve difficulties in our writing can teach us how to solve difficulties in our lives.

Getting Published and the Business of Writing

o you've mustered all your inspiration and all your skills. You've written something that you think is really good. How do you get it published? There are numerous books that give an expanded answer to that question. Most large book stores have a wide selection. Scott Edelstein's *30 Steps to Becoming a Writer and Getting Published* is helpful. You might also try *The Complete Idiot's Guide to Getting Published* by Sheree Bykofsky and Jennifer Basye Sander.

The following is my condensed explanation. At bottom, there are only two ways: without or with an agent. If you don't have an agent, your only choice is to send your manuscript directly to a publisher. For short stories, this practice is common, except for the highest-paying, so-called slick (because they used coated paper) magazines, *Playboy* and *The New Yorker*, to name a couple, where the competition among writers is so fierce that an agent who knows the editors is almost essential. Otherwise, an agent isn't necessary to send a story to a literary magazine on a university campus (most pay only by giving you copies of their magazine, by the way) or to pulp magazines, which are so-called because they use a coarse, pulp type of paper. The latter magazines are easily found in super-market magazine areas. They tend to publish genre stories (*Ellery Queen's Mystery Magazine* and *The Magazine of Fantasy and Science Fiction*, for example) and usually pay a few cents a word. You can see why agents don't get involved in this sort of thing. The commission is too small to pay for their time.

For help in contacting a publisher directly, read *Writer's Market*. This is a thick yearly book that, among other things, provides the addresses of various magazine and book publishers, the names of editors, and the type of material they're looking for. Figure out which publishers would be suitable for what you've written. Some have great success with horror and science fiction. Others won't go near those categories. Write a letter that introduces you and the piece you're submitting. Make it less than a page. Explain why you think your work could attract an audience. Michael Larson's *How to Write a Book Proposal* tells you how to do this. Stephen King's *On Writing* also has some excellent tips about query letters. Enclose a portion of the manuscript and a description of the rest. Cross your fingers.

That type of submission used to be called "sending something over the transom," from when doors had ventilation windows (transoms) above them. The expression conjures the image of a manuscript being hurled over the door into the editor's office. In reality, the following is what happens. Your package arrives at the mail room of the publishing house. The editor's assistant collects the editor's mail, opens it, reads your letter, determines that you don't have any relationship with the editor, and instead of passing the manuscript on, puts it in a storage area, affectionately known as the slush pile. Enterprising assistants, eager to become editors, sometimes spend their lunch hours browsing through the slush pile. They look at the first few pages of each manuscript in the hopes of finding an incident, a tone, something that attracts their attention enough to read further. Those manuscripts that don't meet this quick review get a "thanks but this doesn't meet our present needs" form letter. If you want the manuscript back, enclose a stamped, self-addressed return mailer. Manuscripts that are handwritten, typed in italics, or typed single-spaced are automatically rejected. Those that are on anything but standard white paper are tossed as well (no colored paper, please, and none of that crinkly bond stuff). One of my publishers allowed me to browse through a slush pile. You have no idea how bad most of the manuscripts are: awful grammar, incorrect format (see *Formatting and Submitting Your Manuscript*, by Jack and Glenda Neff and Don Prues, for the proper one), corrections all over the pages, which reek of cigarette smoke. Sometimes it isn't necessary to read something. A manuscript's appearance (and odor) can scream that the writer is an amateur.

On rare occasions, an assistant will find a manuscript that's encouraging. The assistant will take it to an editor, who might look at it but who in all likelihood will tell the assistant to see how much work the manuscript needs. Now your fate depends on the amount of spare time, nights, weekends, the assistant is willing to spend on your manuscript. Some famous novels are said to have survived the slush pile (I heard that Colleen McCullough's *The Thorn Birds* is one of them). For the most part, though, you can see how chancy this form of submission is.

For the best odds, you need an agent. How do you get an agent? There's an old joke that you can't get a publisher without an agent but you can't get an agent without already having been published. In reality, many agents are on the lookout for promising talent. *Writer's Market* has a list of agents and the type of fiction they like to work with. So does *Writer's Digest's* yearly *Guide to Literary Agents*. Read Lori Perkins's *The Insider's Guide to Getting an Agent*. In addition, take a look at Richard Curtis's *How To Be Your Own Literary Agent*, the title of which is humorously misleading since Curtis, a top agent, implies that, if you try to represent yourself, you have a fool for a client.

One way of selecting an agent is by excluding others. For the most part, an agent who deals with New York publishers but doesn't live in the New York area has a disadvantage. I prefer an agent who knows the editors to whom he or she is submitting, who occasionally shares breakfast, lunch, or dinner with them, who runs into them at the Literary Guild's annual cocktail party, in short someone who's more than a name on a letter or a voice on the phone. Send a brief, carefully written letter along with a portion of the manuscript. I say "portion" because there are many more agents than publishers. Finding one who likes your work and whose manner *you* like can take numerous submissions. To minimize your expenses, send the first act, plus a synopsis of the

remainder (and, as always, a stamped, self-addressed return enve-
lope). Believe me, if the agent likes that first act and the synopsis,
he or she will definitely ask for more.

An alternative, easier, cheaper method is to use email to submit
your query letter and part of your novel. Some agents and editors
are still traditional enough that they won't accept electronic
submissions, but most no longer have a problem with that. But
bear in mind that these are busy people who receive several
hundred emails a day. If your letter is wordy and unfocused, they'll
hit the delete key immediately whereas with a hard-copy letter
they might actually skim to the bottom of the page.

An agent who agrees to represent you will probably ask you to
sign an agreement in which you give that agent exclusive rights to
try to sell your work in exchange for a percentage of whatever
money the agent earns for you. When I first started, that commission (for the domestic market) was 10 percent. For most agents, it
is now 15 percent. A reputable agent will not charge a fee until a
sale has been made. The agent receives the money from the
publisher, deducts the commission plus certain expenses, such as
copying costs (increasingly rare in the age of email submissions),
and mails you a check. Any agent who won't read your work
without being paid first should be avoided—a reading fee is not
standard industry practice.

What do you get for the 15 percent? Ideally, a salesperson with
connections and negotiation skills who gives you editorial suggestions, business advice, and psychological boosts. Your agent runs
interference for you with your publisher, makes sure payments
arrive on schedule, and generally looks after your literary welfare
while you're busy writing. In the best circumstances, your agent
also becomes your friend. Seen from that perspective, the 15
percent is a bargain.

Let's say you don't have an agent and an editor picks your manuscript off the slush pile, recognizes its brilliance, and makes you an
offer. Your natural impulse is to jump up and down excitedly, ask
"Where's the money?" and sign the contract. Stop after you've

jumped up and down. Tell the editor that you're thrilled to have your book accepted but that you're so new to the business, you'd like to have an agent look at the contract. Instead of being insulted, the editor will understand. Indeed the editor should even encourage you to get an agent. I assure you that, with an offer from a publisher, you won't have any trouble getting an agent to represent you.

The money you're being offered (which I'll get to in a minute) isn't the only reason you need an agent. The contract will have various clauses that might be troublesome in the future if not examined now. Richard Curtis's book explains most standard clauses in a contract and which are the troubling ones. Consider this clause, for example: In exchange for 50 percent of the proceeds, the publisher will attempt to sell your book to foreign publishers. Sounds reasonable on the surface. A while ago, you were a desperate author, and now not only has your book been accepted but the publisher is talking about selling it overseas. The problem is that most agents either handle foreign sales themselves or ask an overseas agent to do it for them, and the fee they charge is usually at least half what the publisher wants.

Here are some other clauses that need to be negotiated. Audio rights: Has the publisher retained these, or are you allowed to sell the audio rights elsewhere, receiving additional money? The same with electronic publishing rights. What about a guaranteed advertising budget? What about the right to be consulted about the design of your book's cover? There are any number of contractual matters that an agent knows to look at but that a newcomer doesn't.

Let's talk about money. The publisher pays you what's called an advance. That's an abbreviation of "advance against royalties." For beginning writers, the advance is usually a conservative estimate based on the number of copies that the publisher thinks it can sell. The royalty rate is usually 10 percent of the cover price of the hardback. So if hardback of your book sells for $25, you're entitled to $2.50 on each copy sold (best-selling writers get 15 percent of the hardback price, and sometimes higher). The standard royalty rate on a mass market paperback is 8 percent, but it climbs if you're a best-selling sensation and the publisher wants to stop you from going to another publisher that'll offer you more.

Don't expect to have huge advances thrown at you. A first novelist is lucky to sell ten thousand copies. Do the math. If the cover price is $25 and the royalty rate is 10 percent and if you manage to sell ten thousand hardbacks, that's $25,000 you're entitled to. But the publisher isn't going to assume you'll sell ten thousand copies. A cautious advance would be $12,500 or less.

If you sell enough books to earn a royalty that exceeds your advance, you'll receive extra money down the road at six-month (spring and fall) or yearly intervals when the publisher sends you a statement about sales. These royalty statements can be baffling—another good reason to have an agent, someone to translate the hieroglyphics for you. The book-club money, if you're lucky enough to get selected, is usually split with the publisher. Also, it counts against your advance so that if you don't sell enough copies in book stores to justify your advance, the money from the book club helps to make up the difference.

But your book hasn't been published yet. Having labored to write the manuscript, you now must labor further to move it through the production process. Your editor will tend to fit into one of two categories. The first is the big-picture editor who sees manuscripts in general terms—whether the story is interesting, whether it's marketable, and so on. The pesky details, such as fixing awkward sentences and clumsy scenes, are left to somebody farther along in the production process (I'll get to that person in a minute). The other kind is a "line editor" for whom no detail in the manuscript is too small to be questioned.

You want the latter. You want somebody with eagle eyes who takes the time to catch every problematic moment in your novel. Of course, before you submitted your manuscript, you did your best to fix every problem you could find. Even so, despite your best efforts, suddenly your manuscript comes back with editorial notes all over it—suggestions, queries, paragraphs crossed out, "unclear" written in the margin. I've known writers who get angry. "How dare this so-and-so ruin my masterpiece with these stupid changes?" Don't let yourself react this way. Be grateful for the goodwill. Remind yourself that you worked on the manuscript for an awfully long time and that you were bound to become too familiar with it to spot inevitable problems that crept in. If you pretend you're the editor and see the manuscript from a new perspective, many of the suggestions will begin to make sense. Pretend you're on a crowded swaying train at 7:30 at night, editing the manuscript as you head home to your family after a long day of meetings at the office. Under those circumstances, your editor has plenty of motive to save energy and make only the most crucial comments on your manuscript. A painstaking job of editing is thus a sign of commitment.

Most of the time, my editor's suggestions are so logical that I have no problem accepting them. When I disagree, I have a good reason. To be sure, sometimes an editor's suggestion is flat wrong. Philip Klass/William Tenn once wrote a short story in which, as a joke, one of the characters was never allowed to finish a line of dialogue. The character would say something like, "Well, I think we should—" Instantly, another character would interrupt him. This went on for a dozen uncompleted speeches throughout the story. Evidently, Klass's editor didn't have a sense of humor. When the edited manuscript was returned to Klass, every speech was completed. Obviously, this is a case where you'd be justified in restoring those speeches to their original versions, politely explaining your rationale. At bottom, the decision is yours. It's your story, not the editor's. But be open-minded when considering his or her suggestions.

The next person to look at your manuscript is the copyeditor, the person responsible for finding grammar and spelling mistakes (those that your line editor hasn't already spotted), unfortunate word repetitions, inconsistent punctuation, and contradictory details (a character has blue eyes at the start and brown eyes on page 100). Some authors see copyeditors as a nuisance, but I view them as my salvation, as my last chance to catch mistakes that somehow get past everyone else and will haunt me if they appear in the published book.

Here's an example. I read the following sentence at least a hundred times at various stages in the manuscript of *Burnt Sienna*. My wife read it. My domestic agent read it. My foreign agent read it. My Hollywood agent read it. My line editor read it. Only when the manuscript was sent to my copyeditor did I finally get a query, "Do you really want to publish this sentence in its present form?" Here, brave reader, is the sentence in all its glory.

The group got off the plan and split into two groups.

Arrgh! Terrible doesn't describe that sentence. I swear, hand to my heart, after all these years, I do know how to write better than that. A momentary carelessness took possession of me, as it occasionally does every writer. Norman Mailer began *Harlot's Ghost*, a novel about the CIA, with a massive grammar mistake in the first sentence.

On a late-winter evening in 1983, while driving through fog along the Maine coast, recollections of old campfires began to drift into the March mist, and I thought of the Abnaki Indians of the Algonquin tribe who dwelt near Bangor a thousand years ago.

No one spotted the error until the book was in stores. That first sentence was fixed in the second edition. If you don't see the error, look at rule eleven in Strunk and White's popular English-usage book, *The Elements of Style*, a copy of which should always be on your desk. "A participial phrase at the beginning of a sentence must refer to the grammatical subject," those authors point out. In this case, the grammar mistakenly suggests that "recollections of old campfires" are "driving through fog along the Maine coast." If this can happen to Norman Mailer, it can happen to anyone. Pray for an attentive copyeditor.

Having read and corrected your editor's version of the manu-script and then your copyeditor's version, you next must read and correct the initial printed version of your book: the galleys. What you're looking for are spelling errors and dropped sentences that have crept in during the printing process. No matter how keenly you look for those errors, I guarantee that you'll miss some and that readers will point them out to you after the book is in stores. Although you'll be wracked by second thoughts and desperate to improve your prose, the opportunity for rewriting is long past. If you try to cut or add something and those changes result in extra printing costs, you'll need to pay for most of those charges. With no opportunity to be creative, faced with the awful responsibility of having written what you now realize is junk, you despairingly go through each sentence, looking for spelling mistakes. The literary equivalent of those factories I worked in when I was in college, this is deadly dull and dispiriting work. As Vance Bourjaily (*The Man Who Knew Kennedy*) once told me, "By now, you want to wrap the text in butcher's paper, secure it with a stout cord, and kick it all the way to the post office." The words you carefully composed barely make sense. You can't imagine why you wrote such a boring book. You become convinced that reviewers will have no trouble seeing how inept you are.

At least promoting the book will take your mind off the impending reviews. If you're a first-time novelist, you get to expe-rience the torture of sitting by yourself in a remote corner of a bookstore, a stack of your masterpiece before you, a pen in your hand, an earnest look on your face, praying, swearing to heaven that you'll mend your vicious ways and become a decent person, doing multiple acts of charity, if only, please Lord, if only some-body comes over and actually buys your book. In my early days as a novelist, I was at signings in which n-o-t a s-o-u-l showed up. The clerks took pity on me and drew straws to decide which one of them would come over and buy my book, the only one I sold. Now that I've been around a while, thank God I've acquired some fans (bless you all!), so the agony of that kind of signing doesn't happen anymore. But I've endured other kinds of horrors.

One that comes to mind involved a publicity tour along the East Coast. Halfway through, I was driven two hundred miles from Washington, DC, to a remote book store on Chesapeake Bay, which I was assured was first-rate, with a lot of loyal customers and a staff dying to promote my fiction. Because of heavy traffic, an escort hired by my publisher took five hours to drive to the store. All the while the sky got darker and the wind got stronger until, when we finally arrived, a hurricane arrived as well. Trapped for hours in the mostly deserted store, accompanied by five clerks, the store's manager, and my escort, the windows trembling from the wind, the parking lot invisible in the torrents, the lights going out, I was assured that the signing had been widely promoted, that hundreds of people had phoned the store about it, that posters had been hung up all over town, that leaflets had been handed out, that huge quantities of books were in stock, and that this would surely have been the best darned signing in the store's history if only it hadn't been for this gosh-danged hurricane. Substitute earthquake, final game of the World Series, election day, prison escape; it's all happened to me. I once went on an eight-city tour in which not one store had copies of the book I was promoting because a flood had destroyed the warehouse containing all the boxes of my books.

My most bizarre publicity-tour experience occurred at a large book store in Cincinnati, Ohio. That city's airport is in Kentucky, requiring me to take a taxi across the river that separates the states. I'd been to a dozen cities in the previous two weeks and was understandably disoriented when I peered through the taxi's front window at what, in the dusk, looked suspiciously like the Brooklyn Bridge.

"What I'm seeing can't be true. That looks like the Brooklyn Bridge," I told the taxi driver.

"It *is* the Brooklyn Bridge."

I've been on the road too long, I thought. I've finally lost my mind. "*But isn't this Cincinnati?*" I've got amnesia, I thought. Dear God, I've promoted the book in so many cities that I went through Cincinnati without even knowing it, and now I'm in Brooklyn, which isn't even on the tour.

"That's right," the taxi driver said. "This is Cincinnati."

"Then how can that be the Brooklyn Bridge?"

"Because the guy who built the Brooklyn Bridge practiced here first."

In that spirit of unreality, here's what happened at my Cincinnati book signing. My publisher had succumbed to a fit of generosity and given the store manager two hundred dollars to make my signing festive. The publisher's idea was to have pizzas and soft drinks on hand. Customers who happened to be in the store and didn't know my work from Heidegger's happily munched pepperoni slices and drank root beer while I stood before them, trying to make them believe that their lives would be immeasurably enriched if they bought my fabulously entertaining novel (or modest words to that effect).

As I continued my speech, I noticed movement to my right and turned to see a thin young man with a closely cropped beard unpacking large metal containers. Assuming he was one of the store's maintenance workers, I redirected my attention to my pizza-munching audience, but when metal clanged to my right, I turned again, this time seeing the young man attach a microphone to a stand. He took a guitar from a case, hitched it around his shoulders, and proceeded to favor the crowd with his rendition of "Puff, the Magic Dragon." The store's manager, it turned out, had decided to make my signing even more festive than anyone could have imagined by using some of the pizza and soft drink money to pay his folk-singer cousin to put on a show. Unfortunately, the cousin hadn't been told about my signing and considered me to be a rude interference with his musical debut. As the audience tapped its feet and hummed to the tune, I told them about my main character, a man who'd assumed a hundred identities, while the bearded young entertainer launched into the second chorus of "Puff, the Magic Dragon." A hefty, steely-eyed man in the audience set down his pizza slice and approached me, whispering in my ear that he was an assassin for a secret government agency and did I want him to kill the folk singer.

"No," I said. "I don't think that'll be necessary."

"You're sure? It won't be any trouble."

"No, really, don't bother."

"Just remember I'm here for you."

"I appreciate it."

"Great pizza."

"Thanks."

Meanwhile, the folk singer kept droning, "Puff, the Magic Dragon."

Going on a publicity tour is a little like what the Army says will happen to you if you sign up. You'll see the world, or at least a lot of the United States. In a blur. I once did an evening book signing in San Francisco, after which my escort hurried me to the San Francisco airport to catch a plane to Los Angeles. As the escort drove away, I smiled and waved, carried my luggage into the terminal, and discovered that I was supposed to be at the *other* airport, the one across the bay in Oakland. After this unfortunate confusion was settled, I arrived in Los Angeles at 1 a.m. I got up at 6:30 for an 8:00 speech to a group of bookstore managers. I was then rushed to the airport for a flight to Denver, where I gave a noon speech to a group of bookstore managers, after which I was rushed to the airport for a flight to Phoenix, where I gave a dinner speech to a group of bookstore managers. The next morning, at 7:00, I was on a flight to Houston, where I did eleven back-to-back interviews, gave a speech at a signing, and hurried to the airport for a flight to Atlanta. All those flights increase the risk that check-in luggage will get lost, so the experienced author learns to live out of carry-on luggage for weeks on end, with emergency supplies FedExed from home. Ah, the glamour.

The most revealing moment in my many publicity tours happened in a cold northern state during winter. I went to a large wholesaler warehouse that sells paperbacks to airports, drug stores, supermarkets, and convenience stores throughout a multistate region. The manager took me into his office, where he proceeded to prepare his best-seller list. You know those lists you see in airports, drug stores, and supermarkets. They usually have fifteen paperback titles, but the lists don't relate to actual sales. They're prepared six months in advance based on what seems likely to be popular. Most of the slots are reserved for brand-name authors (King, Grisham, Clancy, Steele, Cornwell, and so on). But sometimes fate determines success. On that particular morning, I watched the manager spread covers across his desk, arranging the titles. Number 8 kept giving him trouble. There were too many covers that emphasized blue. The lack of contrasting colors offended his aesthetic eye, so he shuffled through the numerous covers that various publishers had sent him, and for no other reason than that the cover was red and that the book (about which he'd never heard a thing) was a legal thriller, a type of story he liked, he made that book number 8 for his upcoming best-seller list.

But that wasn't my most revealing moment about how arbitrary the book business can be. No, that revealing moment came when the manager gave me a final guided tour of the immense warehouse, which was toasty warm despite a snow storm outside. We walked past towering row after row of boxes of books until we reached the back of the warehouse, where flames flickered and a roar grew louder. We had come to the source of the warehouse's toasty warmth—a massive, open-doored furnace. To understand the point of this story, you need to be aware that the book business is one of the few that allows its wholesale and retail outlets to return all unsold stock for a full refund. For hardbacks, warehouses and stores must return the actual books. For paperbacks, only the covers need to be returned to receive credit. What happens to the books whose covers were torn off? That's what I was looking at, pile after pile of coverless paperbacks being thrown into the furnace to heat the warehouse.

"This is where your books'll end up some day, too," the manager told me. Years later, I still can't imagine his motive for saying that.

Was he trying to be funny? Was he by nature cruel? Whatever, he spoke the truth. When you stare into the mouth of that furnace and see all those books on fire, you forget about fame as a reason for writing.

Money isn't a reason either, as we agreed, but it does pay the bills, so it's time we addressed the subject. The key to sustaining a career is managing your income. A while back, I mentioned that my 1972 *First Blood* advance was $3,500, out of which came a 10 percent agent's commission and income taxes. Obviously, that wasn't enough to support my family if I wanted to resign from the university and write full time. As it happened, I loved teaching and wouldn't resign until many years later when I no longer had the energy to sustain two full-time professions. Soon, *First Blood*'s hardback publisher negotiated a deal with a paperback publisher, my share of which was $42,500. Do you think I now could afford to leave the university if I'd wanted to? No way. Watch how the money disappeared. I deducted the 10 percent agent's commission: $4,250. That left $38,250. From that, I deducted the then-40 percent combined federal and state income tax: $15,300. That left $22,950. A far cry from $42,500, but more than the $13,500 I earned as an assistant professor. Nonetheless, more of the money disappeared.

When you receive income as a writer, the IRS generally considers you self-employed, which means that, instead of an employer deducting your taxes from each paycheck, you need to do it yourself, paying it in four quarterly installments: April, June, September, and January. The tax authorities assume that most people have a steady income. Thus, if you earned $38,250 in the present year, it takes for granted that you'll earn the same amount next year, which means that you need to set another $15,300 aside for your quarterly payments, and those payments begin right now. If you don't earn $38,250 next year, you'll get the money back as an overpayment on your taxes. If you do earn $38,250, your tax liability is covered, although you'll need to set aside another $15,300 for your further quarterly payments. No matter how you calculate it, the tax authorities always hold your money months ahead of your obligation to file a tax return. This might not sound fair, but it's the law, and the IRS charges you a penalty if you fail to pay exactly what you owe. You might ask, "How does any writer earn a living in a system that works like that?" The answer is, the first year you earn significant money is the worst in terms of the tax consequences. After that year, you tend to keep pace with your quarterly payments. You also need to make payments for social security and Medicare.

The bottom line? From the moment you earn any money, keep a record of your income. Save receipts for any expenses that pertain to your writing. That means anything to do with your computer (or however you write), paper, copying costs, mailing costs, books, long-distance phone calls—any writing-related expenditure. If you traveled somewhere to do research, the money you spent is a legitimate deduction. If you went to New York to meet your publisher and your agent, the business part of your trip is a deduction. Maintain a detailed, clear, complete record of those expenses and your income. Go to a tax consultant. Get professional advice. The consultant's fees are tax deductible.

The best writing-as-a-business advice I ever received came from Philip Klass/William Tenn. He suggested that, if I ever wanted to quit teaching and write full time, I should wait until I had enough savings to support my family at its present level of comfort for two years. "That way, you're not writing scared," he said. "You've got time to let the writing come naturally rather than forcing it."

That's the same advice I give writers who are tempted to quit their day jobs. It's not only a question of having a financial buffer so that you're not writing scared. It's also a question of the uncertainty a writer faces. How can you be sure that your next book will be accepted by a publisher? How can you be certain that you won't get writer's block or that your next book won't take twice as long to write as the first one did? Writing is an ecstatically liberating and fulfilling experience. But the *business* of writing is lonely and at times plain frightening. Think carefully about leaving your day job.

Do it with planning, with enough savings to support yourself (it's harder with a family) at your present level for two years.

Consider the consequences of becoming self-employed. If you work in a factory or an office, there's a good chance that your employer pays some, if not all, of your health insurance and possibly some kind of retirement plan. A lot of people do *not* have those benefits, of course, but for purposes of illustration, let's say you do. Now you're going to quit and become a full-time writer. Without health insurance? Without a pension or 401(k)? Not a good idea. I know it sounds crazy to think about retiring when you're only starting your self-dependent career. But if you don't protect yourself, nobody else is going to. The costs of health insurance and a pension are now your responsibility. Factor these expenses into your decision to quit your day job. Some and perhaps all of your health insurance premiums can be deductible, depending on year-to-year changes in the tax law. A properly set up pension can also be tax deductible. If you have a sufficient level of income, you might want to form an S corporation, which (in too complex a way to explain here) can help your tax situation. But think twice about deducting a home office. As justified as the deduction might be, the IRS tends to use it as an excuse for looking closely at your tax return. See a specialist about these matters. There are many other aspects to the business of writing, particularly when it comes to the movies, but let's save that subject for our next lesson.

Rambo and the Movies

T he year after my agent sold *First Blood* to a hardback
publisher, he also sold that novel to the movies, and from a
business point of view, it's worth explaining the process.
First, you need to understand that the film industry has a cyclical
attitude toward purchasing the movie rights to novels. Some years,
producers have a keen interest in buying novels. Other years, all
they care about is buying what are called "spec" scripts. The "spec"
is short for speculation and basically means that a writer had an
idea for a script and sat down to write it in a state of faith and
hope, without any commitment from a studio to buy it. The
advantage of preferring to look at a spec script is that the studio
can pretty much tell right away whether the story feels like it can
be a movie, whereas with a novel the studio can't really know if it
can be a movie until the book (possibly six hundred or more
pages) is adapted into a screenplay (probably 115 pages), a reduction process known as development.

Sometimes, a lot of adaptations of a novel are needed before a
studio decides whether to put the story in front of the cameras. As
a consequence, the development process can be expensive, and
that's on top of the cost of acquiring the rights to a novel. Seen
from this point of view, spec scripts can save both money and time.
The trouble is that spec scripts tend to deal with familiar themes
and situations, whereas novels often offer something new (unless
the novel is yet another opus about a serial killer). So the studios
tire of buying the same old thing in spec scripts and direct their
attention toward novels. Then the studios tire of the tedious, costly
adaptation process and go back to preferring ready-made spec

scripts. An added factor is that, for the most part, novels that are costly to buy usually don't result in money-making films. The studios take a while before their corporate memory about these failures dims enough for them to start buying novels again.

But let's say that novels are in favor. In that case, studios like to see novels before they're published. A lot of this involves executives wanting to be the first to get something new. After making phone calls to stimulate interest, an agent might submit the novel to only one carefully chosen producer at a time, swearing each not to show it to anyone else (lots of luck), or the agent might conduct an auction and send copies of a manuscript to as many as fifteen producers at once, giving them the pressure of a deadline—a week and sometimes only a weekend to decide if they want to buy it.

When the manuscript arrives at the producer's office, does that producer shut the door and eagerly read it? No way. The producer has what are called "readers," specialists whose opinions the producer trusts and who earn their living by reading manuscripts in a hurry, summarizing the plots on a page or two, and recommending whether the book should be acquired or not. These days, the going rate for this service is around $300. Sometimes, these readers need to assess three or four books in one weekend. (A friend who worked in this capacity was also a bartender at the same time.) Astonishing though it is, many of the most important decisions in the film business are made by people who are paid virtually nothing and have no accountability but wield enormous influence.

Why don't movie producers read the projects submitted to them? Let me tell you about an enlightening morning I once experienced on the Warner Bros. lot. This was back in the late 1970s, when I was still innocent. I'd written a script about an architect going through a mid-life crisis. In his youth, he was the leader of a motorcycle gang. He got in trouble with the law, was given the choice of either entering the military or going to reform school, chose the military, mended his life, and is now extremely successful. But memories of those motorcycles, the thrills of his youth, nag at him. Something's missing in his life, and to find it, he rejoins the motorcycle culture, a genteel part of it at least. He participates in races and such, feeling young again until he comes in conflict with a modern motorcycle gang, a criminal one that drags him down into a nightmare of violence.

My agent submitted the script to a producer, who to protect the guilty shall go nameless. The producer liked it, thought it would be ideal for motorcycle-enthusiast Steve McQueen, then paid my air fare to come out and discuss the script. In the process of our brief relationship, the producer suggested that I spend a morning in his office, watching him conduct business. It would be instructive, he suggested. Boy, was it ever.

This was how the morning went. His assistant, who had a tiny office next to the producer's palatial one, waited for the phone to ring.

The assistant answered, "Good morning. This is Mr. So-and-so's office . . . I'm sorry. He's not here now. May I have your name?"

After she hung up, the producer called to her, "Who was that?"

"Bob [fill in the blank]."

"*Him?*" the producer asked. "I wonder what *he* wants."

So the producer called someone who knew the man who'd just phoned the producer. The producer schmoozed for a while and then said, "Oh, by the way, Bob [fill in the blank] got in touch. Do you have any idea what he's doing these days?"

The producer listened for a while, getting the scoop, nodding sagely. "Thanks. I owe you. How's the wife? We should get together one of these days."

As he hung up, the phone rang in the other room.

The assistant said, "This is Mr. So-and-so's office . . . He's not here now. May I have your name?"

The producer asked, "Who was that?"

"Ralph [fill in the blank]."

"I wonder what *he* wants." The producer tapped numbers on his phone. Schmooze, schmooze, schmooze. "Say, Ralph [fill in the blank] called a while ago. Have you any idea what he's doing these days?"

And on it went all morning, a round-robin of phone calls with nobody talking directly to anyone else. Sometimes the people the producer phoned wouldn't take his calls, just as *he* wasn't taking calls. No doubt, those people who refused his call were phoning other people to try to learn what the producer wanted.

Madness. The movie business is based on maneuvering and insecurity masked by gigantic personalities. Most producers have the skill of the Great Gatsby, able to make you feel instantly that you are the most important person in their lives. I once met a producer whose seductive first words to me were, "David, what in the world do you most want?" What was I to answer? A yacht? A villa on the Riviera? World peace? An end to famine and pestilence? Hell, no. My answer was, "For you to make this movie."

Calculating and outguessing can be busy work. It leaves little time for anything as mundane as reading. Anybody can do that. Hire someone. The one- or two-page condensation of the book that the reader submits to the producer with a recommendation of whether to buy or reject it is called "coverage." One of my favorite Hollywood jokes is a story attributed to Pat Conroy (*The Prince of Tides*). After a studio bought one of Conroy's novels, the executive in charge of the project met him, put an arm around him, and told him confidentially, "You're an absolutely great writer. One of the all-time best. The coverage on your book moved me to tears."

Are you getting the idea? The movie business is frustrating and weird with its own unique standards of behavior, particularly when it comes to dealing with writers. As one executive said, "Writers? What's the big deal? All they do is put one word after another." That producer who let me stay in his office for a morning? We had a verbal agreement that I'd receive an option of $10,000 while he set up the deal with McQueen. But then it turned out that McQueen had experienced some kind of breakdown. The actor was seventy-five pounds overweight, had a beard and long hair that made him look like a cave man, and was fixing his motorcycle in his living room while he drank beer all day and watched soap operas on television. Moreover, the actor was charging a million dollars just to read any scripts submitted to him, and those scripts needed to be left at the gas station near his Trancas Beach home. A scam artist because of his troubled youth, the actor was rumored never to look at those scripts but to charge the million dollars anyhow. With McQueen out of the question, the producer stalled on sending me a contract while he took the script all over Hollywood trying to get other actors interested in it. But not many actors were suited for that role, and when the producer failed, he told me that the project wasn't going to happen and walked away.

"But what about my $10,000 dollars?" I asked.

"Sorry. We don't have a contract."

The creep had given me his word that the contract would arrive any day. Meanwhile, he'd acted as if the script belonged to him. He shopped it all over town. It become old news, and believe me, in Hollywood there's nothing worse than old news. The producer hadn't only cheated me out of $10,000; he'd ruined my agent's chance of ever getting the script sold to anyone else (it never did sell).

Let's say your agent phones to say that a studio wants to buy the film rights to your book. You start imagining that you own a beach house at Malibu. You see yourself in a Porsche driving onto the Paramount lot where every producer, director, and star treat you like the swellest, smartest, most talented person in the business. Stop a second. First, your agent hasn't received a contract for you. All the agent has is someone's word, contingent on various conditions, that the studio wants to buy your book. When the contract finally does arrive, it might contain clauses that are punitive to you and maddeningly complicated to remove. Negotiations for one of my books once lasted a year and a half from when the studio agreed to buy the novel until the final contracts were delivered. The money didn't arrive until two months after that. What if I'd been counting on it to pay my mortgage?

In fact, that once happened to a writer I know. He had a big deal in the works. Assuming it would go through, he quit his day job, bought a huge house, got an expensive car, and generally lived like a king—until the deal fell through and he had to declare bankruptcy. An oral agreement means nothing. A contract means nothing. I wish I could give names in the following story. A famous writer who's a friend once had to spend a quarter million dollars in legal fees to straighten out a contract that promised him half that amount. The head of the prestigious studio that caused so much trouble then phoned my friend to suggest that they work on another project.

"After all the money I lost on this project, not to mention the aggravation? I don't think so," my friend said.

"All right, all right, I admit it," the executive said. "My contracts aren't worth shit, but I promise, my word is as good as gold."

Right. When you get the movie money in your hand, *then* you can think about doing something with it (like putting it in the bank instead of spending it).

Unless your agent is an expert in the movie business, whose executives seem to change positions daily, you're going to need Hollywood representation. Your East Coast agent will help you select one. Don't try to do it yourself. You're a babe in the woods. If you're "hot" as they say "out there," the folks on the West Coast will promise you anything and eat you for lunch. If you're not hot, nobody will answer your phone calls. For that matter, even if you *are* hot, producers don't always answer your phone calls.

If you really want something to do with the movie business, don't approach it with, excuse the pun, stars in your eyes. Learn about its intricacies. Read the two principal industry magazines: *Variety* and *The Hollywood Reporter* (just as you should read *Publishers Weekly* to learn what's happening in the book business). Read William Goldman's *Adventures in the Screen Trade* and its follow-up, *Which Lie Did I Tell? Further Adventures in the Screen Trade*. Read his *The Big Picture: Who Killed Hollywood? And Other Essays.* Read anything he writes about the film industry. Another benefit of reading *Adventures in the Screen Trade* is that it contains Goldman's Oscar-winning screenplay for *Butch Cassidy and the Sundance Kid* (in case you've never seen a screenplay).

Educate yourself. If you want to write screenplays in addition to novels, make sure your format is correct. Studios don't read scripts that look odd (just as publishers don't read single-spaced manuscripts on colored paper). Study Rick Reichman's *Formatting Your Screenplay*. If you use a word processor, consider buying one of the screenplay-formatting programs.

Basically, there are two types of movie deals. The first is called an option. In this case, your agent and the studio agree on a purchase price. But the studio doesn't want to pay that amount right away. It's not sure it can get the right director and star, for example. So instead of buying the novel outright, the studio options your novel, that is, pays a smaller amount in exchange for the right to develop your novel into a screenplay during a specific period of time: a year or two. If the studio gets the right director and star before the deadline, it pays you the remainder of the purchase price and the film rights belong to the studio. If the studio doesn't combine the right elements before the deadline, you get to keep the money the studio gave you and take the book somewhere else.

In the second type of movie deal, the studio gives you the full amount of the purchase price and owns the movie rights. Do your best to have a clause added to the contract, stipulating that, if the movie hasn't been made in ten years, the film rights for the book revert to you. That is sometimes called "turnaround," and it sounds like a good deal, but unfortunately the studio will insist on its own clause, stipulating that, if the rights revert to you and you sell the book somewhere else, you need to repay the studio what it paid you, plus its expenses in trying to develop the script, plus interest, plus overhead. These charges are often so onerous that the book's film rights are too expensive for anyone to want to acquire them in turnaround.

In the case of *First Blood*, the film deal was an outright sale. The verbal agreement was in early 1972, just before the novel was published. The purchase price was $90,000, a lot of money then (still is, but not in the movie business). After the $9,000 agent's fee was deducted, I got to keep the rest, except for what the tax authorities wanted. But that money and the paperback money were yet to be received. All I had in my hand was the $3,500 book advance, minus the deductions I mentioned. After flying to New York to meet the publisher, I think I had a thousand dollars left. And then my agent suggested that it would be a good idea for an attorney to go over the *First Blood* film contract.

"Attorney?" I asked. "How much is *he* going to cost?"

"Five hundred dollars."

"Five hundred!" For someone earning $13,500 as an assistant professor, this was a ton of cash.

"I think it would be well spent," the agent said.

So I reluctantly agreed, and a month later, the attorney came back with his suggestions.

"David, you now have profit participation not only in the *First Blood* movie but also in any sequels."

"Sequels?" I cringed, convinced that I'd wasted my hard-to-come-by money. "But almost every major character's dead at the end of the novel. How can there be sequels?"

"David, you don't know what Hollywood can do with a novel. Maybe everybody'll live. Maybe the story'll end up as a musical comedy on a submarine. By the way, I also asked for profit participation on any merchandise associated with the film."

"Merchandise?"

"Dolls. Lunch boxes. Television cartoons. Who knows? Anything's possible. That's why you hired me. To predict the future."

"Dolls? Lunch boxes? Impossible!"

In addition to the eventual dolls and lunch boxes, there was in fact a half-hour television Rambo cartoon series. When Rambo wasn't saving democracy from Third World dictators, he sat around the forest, talking to animals. Weird, but at least it had Jerry Goldsmith's wonderful music.

As long as I raised the subject of profit participation, let's analyze its intricacies. First, let's understand the basic economics of the industry. A company spends $100 million to make a movie. That's the budget. The company then has to market and distribute it. If the company is a huge studio, it can accomplish those tasks on its own. But if the company is small, with limited resources, it undergoes the extra expense of hiring a marketer and distributor. The latter prepares prints of the film and delivers them to the theaters. The cost per print varies, starting around $1,500. A big budget film might open in at least five thousand theaters, with a minimum print cost of $7.5 million. Meanwhile, the marketing department prepares trailers to be shown in theaters. It creates media ads and pays to have them appear. It conducts publicity tours. For a $100 million film, the marketing and distribution costs might be another $100 million.

Then the exhibitors enter the equation. They make a complex deal with the distributor in which for the first week each theater might get ten cents on the dollar, for the second week twenty cents, for the third week thirty cents, and so on until the theater gets ninety cents on the dollar. The point is, not all the proceeds from ticket sales go to the studio that made the film. The theaters want something for themselves.

So when you hear that a film earned $150 million in domestic box-office receipts, remember that the theaters take a cut of that, and so does the distributor. A picture that costs $100 million and earns $150 million at the box office doesn't have a profit of $50 million. It's deep in the hole. The basic rule is, multiply a film's budget by three (and sometimes four). That's how much the film needs to earn before it can break even after the theaters and the distributor deduct what is owed to them and then pass the remaining money to the production company. These days, the money from foreign sales, television fees, and home-video profits is so great that the picture I just mentioned has a chance to break even, assuming that it did as well overseas as it did domestically.

With that understood, we can talk about profits. There are two kinds: gross and net. If you're Steven Spielberg, your profit partici-pation comes off the top, the gross, every dollar earned at the box office. If you're a lowly writer, however, your profit participation (the standard is 5 percent) comes off the net after Steven gets his cut, the theaters take their cut, the distributor takes its cut, and the studio recoups the money it put into the picture. But that's not all. Before the studio declares a profit, it deducts a hefty overhead fee and its own distribution fee, as much as 40 percent. Seen in this context, profits are like the horizon—they recede infinitely. On occasion, a film is so outrageously successful that it earns a profit in spite of the system's best effort to keep it in the red. If you manage to sell a novel to the movies and you get profit participation, don't hold your breath, and don't be surprised by the magic of the accounting process. Still, hope springs eternal. In my own case, I did receive profit payments from the Rambo movies and from NBC's *Brotherhood of the Rose* miniseries. Miracles can happen.

But we're assuming that your book will actually get filmed. For every thousand books purchased by the studios, only a handful ever get made into movies, and only a handful of that handful is successful at the box office. There are too many barriers. Trends change. One year, comedies are hot, and action movies are passé. The next year, action movies have legs, as they say in the business, with horror movies gaining ground. Hollywood tends to go with the current sensation, and your book might not be part of the trend. Then, too, actors and directors can lose interest. Worse, your project can get stuck in committee meetings, with all the participants needing desperately to pretend they're worth the money they earn by voicing opinions about the latest script until the story (if it still resembles your book) is mired permanently in what's called development hell.

In that regard, one of my worst development experiences involved *The Fifth Profession*. That novel is about an American and a Japanese executive protector (sophisticated bodyguards who protect the powerful). On a nightmarish mission, each seemed to see the other beheaded. A year later, they discovered that each was alive. How could this be possible? The plot compelled the two protectors, wary of each other, to join forces and eventually become friends (much like the relationship between the United

States and Japan in those years) as they struggled to find the secret behind their false memories.

The Fifth Profession was sold outright to a major studio in 1989. I asked the producer assigned to the project if I could do the screenplay. Such a request is almost always declined because of an industry attitude that novelists aren't good adapters of their work. The prejudice has merit. Most novelists aren't good screenwriters. They frequently can't force themselves to cut favorite but marginal scenes in order to condense their novels into screenplays. Moreover, they're conditioned to using a multi-sensual technique in their stories and can't adjust to restricting themselves to details of sight and occasionally of sound.

I wasn't surprised, then, when the producer said that he wanted someone else to do the screenplay. No harm in asking, however. I went on to other projects and occasionally got progress reports from the producer. That courtesy is a rarity, by the way. Most of the time, when you sell a book's film rights, you're ignored from the moment you sign the contract. If you finally lose patience and decide to phone the producer, a receptionist will say that he or she is out of the office and ask for your phone number, promising to get back to you. Sand will become pearls in oysters faster than the producer will return your call. You're not necessary anymore.

But in this case, courtesy prevailed. The producer phoned every few months to explain that the screenwriters he hired weren't giving him the approach he wanted. He sent me one of the scripts, which was a more or less literal adaptation of the story, with the difference that arbitrary car chases, explosions, and elaborate gun fights had been crammed in.

"So-and-so [he mentioned the name of the studio head] says he won't greenlight the project unless I turn it into a franchise." Translation: The studio won't allow the picture to be made unless there's a way to do three or four big pictures with the same characters, in the manner of the *Lethal Weapon* series.

"Your Japanese guy," the producer went on, "dies in the book and in all these scripts. We can't have a franchise unless he lives. Plus, we'd like this to have the look and feel of James Bond so it has Bond's legs." Meaning, Bond's box-office longevity.

Six months later, he sent me a new script, with an enthusiastic note that finally he'd found a writer who'd cracked the problem.

The new script had nothing to do with false memory and the symbolic relationship of the American and Japanese. The story was now set in the future and involved a wacko billionaire who used his space satellites to disrupt the world's oil supply. His evil network was based in a dead volcano in Japan, where our intrepid heroes led a band of black-clad ninja warriors in a daring attack that required them to enter the volcano by sliding down ropes.

Stunned, I phoned the producer, who amazed me by taking the call. "The James Bond people are going to sue you," I said.

"What are you talking about?"

"The entire climax of this script comes from *You Only Live Twice*. The gimmick of the space satellites was used in a couple of other Bond movies and—"

"*You Only Live Twice*? I don't remember it."

"That's the one in which Sean Connery pretends to be Japanese."

"Connery? The only Bond movies I saw when I was growing up starred Roger Moore."

But the new scriptwriter saw the Connery movies, that was certain. In fact, it turned out that—told to make *The Fifth Profession* like a Bond movie—he'd rented every Bond movie regardless of who was the star and crammed them together into a melange that favored *You Only Live Twice*, neglecting to use almost everything in my novel. The project was soon abandoned and reverted to me ten years later, thanks to a "turnaround" clause in the contract, but millions of dollars of overhead charges are now attached to it.

Development hell nearly happened to *First Blood*. Having signed the movie contract, I waited for the film to get made. And waited. And waited. Columbia Pictures had purchased *First Blood* for Richard Brooks (*Elmer Gantry*, *The Professionals*) to write and direct. It was Brooks' idea that the film would end with Rambo and the police chief forced to take cover together when a mob of armed men lost control and shot at everything in sight. As bullets flew, the police chief delivered the script's final line: "None of this would have happened if only we'd tried to understand each other." I have no idea if this line was typical of the script that Brooks submitted a year later to Columbia. I do know that Columbia canceled the project and sold it to Warner Bros., where Martin Ritt was considered as the director and Paul Newman the star. The script treated the policeman as the major character. Presumably Newman was going to portray him, spending a lot of time drinking in the back seat of a police car when he wasn't talking to his reflection in a mirror while urinating in a men's room. (I've seen many weird things in men's rooms, but never a mirror above a urinal.) Meanwhile, Rambo demonstrates the wily arts of the outdoorsman by breaking into a commercial cave and looting the vending machines. A character describes Rambo as "the Bobby Riggs of guerrilla warfare." Terrible.

When Warner Bros. rejected this version, they then hired Sydney Pollack to direct a new script that was tailored for (before he became too fat to be recognizable) Steve McQueen. McQueen, an accomplished biker, was eager to do the motorcycle chase after Rambo escapes from jail. The fatal problem (realized only after six months of development) was that McQueen was in his mid-forties and, in 1975 when this version was being prepared, a Vietnam veteran of that age would have been ludicrous. Back to the drawing board. Ultimately the novel passed through three movie companies and eighteen scripts. Nick Nolte, Clint Eastwood, Robert De Niro, and Michael Douglas were all considered as Rambo.

Then in 1980, two film distributors, Andrew Vajna and Mario Kassar, formed a production company named Carolco. Seeking a project, they happened upon a *First Blood* script by William Sackheim and Michael Kozoll (the latter a co-creator of *Hill Street Blues*). They decided that with modification the story would play well in America. More important, their experience in foreign film markets told them that the movie, if it emphasized action, would attract large audiences around the world.

Provided they found the right actor. At the start of the 1980s, Sylvester Stallone's only financial successful film had been *Rocky*. So when Vajna and Kassar offered Stallone the role, industry observers were skeptical. For that matter, so was Stallone. At the time, he was quoted as saying that he feared *First Blood* would be the most expensive home movie ever made. Much later, he said that it was the film that made the most difference in his career.

To market their film to foreign distributors, Vajna and Kassar assembled a shortened version that contained only action sequences. One of the film's co-stars, Richard Crenna, told me that those distributors expected so little they were close to yawning when they arrived in the screening room. Less than an hour later, when the lights came on, it was like the New York stock exchange, Crenna said, as everybody lunged toward Vajna and Kassar to acquire various overseas rights. As an added marketing ploy, Vajna and Kassar wanted the film to be only ninety-six minutes long, allowing theaters to squeeze in an extra showing each day. The producers also kept the film's dialogue to a minimum, reducing the cost of translations into other languages (and the humorous mistakes that such translations often create). Stallone with a torn shirt, holding a machine gun: That iconic image on the film's poster went beyond words.

In the adaptation process, some changes were made. The novel's locale was shifted from Kentucky to the Pacific Northwest, partly because of the favorable exchange rate between the American and Canadian dollar and because of the financial incentives the Canadian government provides to films that use Canadian locations and personnel. Another reason was that British Columbia's winters are mild—ironically, the production was shut down by a blizzard. Rambo acquired the first name John ("When Johnny comes marching home"). Also he was made less angry and violent (for thematic reasons, he's far more lethal in my novel). On the screen, Rambo throws a rock at a helicopter, causing a demented sharpshooter to fall to his death. Later, Rambo bumps a stolen truck against a pursuing police car filled with gun-blazing deputies; they crash into a car at the side of the road. Neither incident is in the novel. That's the total body count in the film. The police chief—now a stereotypical redneck—is badly wounded but lives. But in my novel the casualties are virtually uncountable. My intent was to transpose the Vietnam War to America. In contrast, the film's intent was to make the audience cheer for the underdog. War is hell as opposed to war is heck.

The most important change between my novel and the film almost didn't occur. I was determined that there be no winners, and so both the police chief and Rambo die. In the novel, Colonel Trautman (Rambo's former commander) blows Rambo's head off with a shotgun. A variation—in which Rambo commits suicide—was filmed. But test audiences found that conclusion too depressing. The film crew returned to Canada to stage a new ending, and Rambo lived. Thus, inadvertently, it was possible to do sequels prompted by the film's success.

And *that* brings me to other business lessons. If you ever sell a novel's movie rights, make sure your contract stipulates that you'll be paid for sequels and remakes. The standard fee for a sequel is half of what you received for the first film; for a remake, it's a third. Sometimes your agent can negotiate a 100 percent fee, but even then, inflation can be your enemy. As I mentioned, in 1972 I received $90,000 for the *First Blood* film rights. Years passed. In 1984, at the start of photography on the second film, whose budget was $27 million, I received . . . divide by two . . . the grand total of (drum roll) $45,000. I received the same low sum for the third movie, which had a budget of $67 million. And the same for the fourth movie, which was released twenty-six years after the first one. What's the moral? There isn't one. I've never heard of a writer getting that sequel payment clause adjusted for inflation. Sometimes you can't avoid getting screwed.

A further business lesson with regard to sequels and remakes is to make sure you retain print control of the characters in your novel. That way, if against all odds the film is actually made and if it's miraculously a hit and if more miraculously there's a sequel, the producers can't hire someone else to trash your characters in a novelization of that sequel. A novelization is a book-length prose embellishment of a screenplay. Because a screenplay has almost no description, only dialogue and lean stage directions, there's plenty of room for amplification. The result is used primarily to promote the film.

God forbid, there might even be a *series* of novelizations about your characters. If you surrender print control when you sell the film rights, you won't have any say about what goes into those novelizations. Think carefully about this. The studio will do everything possible to talk you out of keeping print control. It will threaten to walk away from the deal. If you need the money and you sign the contract without that clause, brace yourself for the possible consequences.

You can, of course, choose to do the novelization yourself. That's what I did when the Rambo producers (with no other choice) asked me to write novelizations for the second and third movies. The characterizations and situations in the scripts, which I did not write, were so paper-thin ("Rambo jumps up and kills this guy." "Rambo jumps up and kills the next guy.") that I thought I owed it to Rambo to put some of my ideas about him into the novelizations, even if those ideas would never be in the films (his antipolitician and anti-Vietnam-War attitudes, for example). Plus, the notion of exploring the novelization mode, of trying something new, appealed to me as a creative exercise. My book version of the first sequel stayed on the *New York Times* best-seller list for six weeks, a rarity.

That sequel, 1985's *Rambo (First Blood Part II)*, was an international box-office sensation. It was intended as action entertainment. But because it dealt with a highly charged political issue (whether or not there were American prisoners of war in Vietnam), it was also extremely controversial (as was the second sequel, 1988's *Rambo III*, which dealt with the Soviet invasion of Afghanistan). President

Reagan didn't seem to mind the controversy, however. One evening, during a televised press conference, he said that he'd seen a Rambo movie the night before and now he knew what to do the next time there was a terrorist hostage crisis. Unfortunately, many people equated the Rambo movies with America's military policy, to the point that while I was on a book tour in Britain in 1986, I read with dismay the London newspaper headline: "U.S. Rambo Jets Bomb Libya."

All this movie success was terrible for my career as a novelist. In the 1970s and early 1980s, *First Blood* was taught in high schools and universities across the country. *English Journal*, a prestigious academic publication for teachers, recommended it for classroom use because of the debate it encouraged about the nature of civil disobedience. For years, I had received favorable letters from teachers telling me how pleased they were by their students' responses to the book. Students who weren't readers took to it and soon were reading anything they could get their hands on.

But by the mid-1980s, when President Reagan made that joke about the Rambo movies, the controversy generated by the films caused teachers to shy away from the book. It was no longer included on reading assignments. The letters stopped. The age of political correctness had arrived. Worse, independent bookstores (which tend to be liberal) grouped the book with the movie (without having read the book) and assumed that I was an ultra right-wing violence-crazed nutcase who wandered his home wearing combat boots and fondling a machine gun, when in fact I'm a registered Democrat and so *non*violent that I carry spiders and insects out of my house rather than kill them because I don't want to invite bad karma. After the President Reagan joke, my novels virtually disappeared from independent book stores. If it hadn't been for the big book chains like Waldenbooks and B. Dalton who continued to stock my books, I'd have been out of business, which is ironic because I'm a longtime supporter of independent book stores. Only by the mid-1990s did independent book stores begin to weaken their anti-Morrell stance and realize that I'm not an ogre.

A lot has happened in the many years since *First Blood* was released as a film in 1982. Carolco, the film company formed by Vajna and Kassar, was a major force in Hollywood until the mid-1990s when a series of box-office disappointments forced the company that made such hits as *Total Recall*, *Terminator 2*, and *Basic Instinct* to declare bankruptcy. Meanwhile, Rambo went on to become so great a part of global popular culture that the character's name was listed as a new word in the *Oxford English Dictionary*.

The Novelist as Marketer

Over the years, I've seen many changes in publishing. One of the biggest involves the industry's attitude toward publicity and marketing. When *First Blood* appeared in 1972, authors weren't expected to do much except write. They entrusted their manuscripts to editors and bided their time, hoping for rave reviews and strong sales. Promotion was simple. The publisher sent enthusiastic letters to reviewers and the media. These letters were mostly plot summaries that accompanied plain paperback versions of the book, known as galleys (what we now call advance readers' copies). Because galleys are expensive, rarely were more than one hundred printed (as opposed to the thousands that are sometimes printed today). If a publisher wanted to show unusually strong support, the galley would be "fancy," with colors and a version of the actual cover. Budget permitting, there might be a launch party and some print advertisements. A few news-paper, radio, and TV interviewers might be persuaded to show interest. That was the campaign, and hardly any of it required authors to participate. In those innocent times, writers tended to follow their natural inclination and remain at home alone in a room, where they concentrated not on promoting their work but on creating it.

There were exceptions. In the nineteenth century, Charles Dickens and Mark Twain went on lengthy tours, attracting enthu-siastic crowds to their public readings. Oscar Wilde made himself a witty presence in London society and was frequently quoted in newspapers. In the 1920s, F. Scott Fitzgerald and his wife Zelda were so conspicuous in Manhattan night life that journalists depicted them as the embodiment of the Flapper era and the Roaring Twenties.

But my favorite in terms of an early master of publicity is Richard Harding Davis (1864-1916). These days, his name draws only blank looks. At the turn of the twentieth century, however, he was one of the most famous authors in the world. As an American newspaperman, he covered every war during his lifetime, witnessing combat in Greece, Cuba, South Africa, Manchuria, and numerous countries in Europe during World War I. In battles in Cuba, he was close enough to hear bullets whizzing over his head and to watch Teddy Roosevelt leading the Rough Riders in a charge near San Juan Hill. He picked up rifles from dead U.S. soldiers and fired at the enemy. During the Boer War, he galloped on horseback to escape exploding artillery shells. In World War I, he was captured by German soldiers, who refused to believe that he was a journalist and almost shot him as a spy.

Through his international newspaper articles, Davis made himself the hero of the events he witnessed. He then recycled his adventures by fictionalizing them in short stories like "Gallegher," creating the reporter-as-hero genre. Countless "stop the presses" short stories, novels, TV programs, and movies are indebted to him. Similarly, one of Davis's numerous bestselling thrillers, *Soldiers of Fortune*, dramatizes a Caribbean civil war, a subject he knew first hand, and while the hero, Robert Clay, is an engineer trying to build a railroad, he strongly resembles Davis. Readers recognized him because his chiseled features and square-shouldered bearing were often featured in magazines, courtesy of his artist friend Charles Dana Gibson whose drawings depicted Davis as the companion of the famous fashion-magazine illustration, the Gibson Girl, which was the epitome of style in the 1890s. Davis never went anywhere without thinking of a way to write about the experience and to emphasize his presence in whatever drama he discovered. The publicity exploits of Stephen Crane, Jack London, and Ernest Hemingway were almost certainly inspired by his astonishing, action-filled life.

These novelists promoted themselves as much as their work. While Hemingway was a literary favorite in the 1920s, he didn't become a popular cultural icon until after he started writing a regular column for *Esquire* in the 1930s, providing details about his adventures as a deep-sea fisherman, big-game hunter, and bullfight *aficionado*. Once referred to as the most photographed man in the world, he made a point of living in glamorous places (Paris, Key West, Cuba, and Sun Valley), even as he pursued danger on an international scale and then wrote novels about it.

Norman Mailer is another example. He helped found *The Village Voice* and thus gained a market for essays that were as much about him as the topic he was supposed to be writing about. The title of one of his collections, *Advertisements for Myself*, makes clear his devotion to publicity, as does his attempt at a much-photographed boxing career. In *The Armies of the Night*, a non-fiction novel, he put himself into the center of the 1967 Vietnam War protest at the Pentagon, complete with his account of how he was arrested and put in jail.

Idealists can argue that the exploits of these authors are irrelevant to their writing, and I agree. From a literary point of view, what matters is what's on the page. Our task is to write the best fiction we can. But readers need to be persuaded to buy a book, and the unhappy fact is that few do so because of literary value alone. Some sort of X factor persuades them, and often it's the strength of the author's public personality.

Because few writers have the charisma or physical stamina to pursue publicity to the degree I've just described, let's switch from macho examples and look at the way a well-known female author handled publicity, a woman who died in 1974 but who continues to influence publishing, not because she was a great writer (which she admitted she wasn't) but because she was a great marketer: Jacqueline Susann. Her novels are scandal-in-show-business sagas whose characters are thinly disguised versions of entertainment stars like Judy Garland, Ethel Merman, and Frank Sinatra. Her most well-known book, *Valley of the Dolls,* was published in 1966 and deals with prescription "uppers" and "downers" in the sensational lives of a model, an actress, and a female singer. It sold more than nineteen million copies (some say thirty million) and continues to attract readers, making it a candidate for the most commercially successful novel of all time.

There's always a market for drugs-and-sex melodramas, but that isn't the only reason Jackie Susann was the first novelist to have three consecutive number-one *New York Times* bestsellers. A former actress, she so understood the value of publicity that she married a press agent, Irving Mansfield. The two of them tirelessly pursued TV talk-show producers and weren't at all daunted when Truman Capote (himself an expert in publicity) told *The Tonight Show*'s Johnny Carson that Jackie's big black wigs and flamboyant clothes made her look like "a truck driver in drag." Capote then apologized to truck drivers. Pouncing on the insult, Jackie and Irving hurried to one of the world's most famous attorneys, Louis Nizer. They threatened lawsuits and were featured in countless newspapers.

According to publishing lore, Jackie more or less invented the multi-city book tour. She and Irving drove across the country, seeking media interviews, then visiting every bookstore they could find and establishing relationships with the staff. The clerks were so impressed by her enthusiasm and commitment that they went out of their way to recommend her books to their customers.

Jackie also influenced the way her books were distributed. In the 1960s, the system was different than it is today. There were numerous wholesaler warehouses, from which truck drivers delivered paperbacks to drug stores, convenience stores, supermarkets, etc. These places sold a lot of books, and the truck drivers who serviced them functioned as *de facto* salesmen. They were on a first-name basis with the store owners and clerks and knew what types of books sold best in various districts. Westerns might be popular in one area while crime stories or science fiction or romances or mainstream fiction might be popular somewhere else. Often, the store owners relied on the truck drivers to choose books for them.

Jackie understood the influence of the drivers and went to as many warehouses as she could, serving coffee and doughnuts early in the morning before the drivers headed out to deliver books. She asked questions about the drivers' background and families while Irving made notes. At holidays or birthdays, the drivers received personal cards in which Jackie referred to the subjects they'd discussed. She became so popular among the drivers that her books were stocked just about anywhere a book could be sold.

But as I indicated, these publicity efforts weren't normal in the publishing world. Only in the mid-1980s, more than a decade after Jackie died, did publishers start sending authors on multi-city book tours, and for a time, the tactic was a huge success. Stores in cities like Cincinnati, Phoenix, Seattle, and Denver usually had access only to local writers, but suddenly fresh authors were available, many of them well-known. Once a week, a reading/signing would occur, with attention from the local media and impressive sales.

Then more authors were sent on tour, and the signings increased to two a week, three a week, four a week, and so on. By the late 1990s, many bookstores throughout the country had a signing every night and sometimes also on weekend afternoons. Not surprisingly, these events became so commonplace that fewer book buyers showed up. At the same time, the local media became overwhelmed. I recall being on tour in Minneapolis, where I sat in the green room of a radio station with six other authors, each of us waiting for our fifteen minutes of air time. We're like planes in a holding pattern on an airport runway, I thought. When my turn came, the interviewer looked sleepless and annoyed, explaining that he hadn't read my novel, that there wasn't time to read *anybody's* novel, given the dozens of writers who came through the station every week. Eventually, publishers were forced to reduce the number of authors they sent on tour. Now it's usually just the most successful writers who get that kind of promotion, and often the result isn't worth the time and expense.

Similarly, in the mid-1980s, the book business followed Jackie's example and began sending authors to wholesaler warehouses to have coffee and doughnuts with the drivers. Unfortunately, those visits also lost their effectiveness, partly because too many authors visited warehouses and partly because the drivers became increasingly less important to the industry. A decline in book sales lead to distributor bankruptcies and consolidation among wholesalers. In the 1960s, there were more than five hundred distributors in the United States. By the mid-1990s, there were significantly fewer, perhaps only a dozen (these days, there are fewer still). Books were shipped over such huge distances that a close relationship no longer existed between the drivers and the stores they serviced. Large delivery companies like UPS received increasingly more contracts to deliver the books until, in 1996, the traditional drivers were dismissed, thus ending what had been an important way to gauge tastes in local areas and to influence which books were sold there. The shockwave through the publishing world is described in detail in Richard Curtis's "The Rise and Fall of the Paperback Market," one of several informative essays about the past and future of U.S. publishing that this long-time agent posts on the Backspace writers' organization website, www.bksp.org.

Despite these changes, many authors view book promotion in terms of a mid-1980s model that Jackie Susann pioneered two decades earlier but that now lacks the power it once had. I don't know any author who'd be disappointed to be offered a multi-city tour, but tours can be expensive, and if organized in a traditional manner, they're a narrow way of promoting a book. In a moment, I'll discuss non-traditional book tours. I'll also suggest several cheaper, potentially more effective ways to promote your fiction. But first you need to understand the way publishing currently works.

Back in the mid-1980s, there were perhaps thirty publishers based in New York City, plenty of opportunities for an agent to place a manuscript. As time passed, consolidation reduced them to a handful of huge corporations. Now, within each of these corporations, several imprints bear the well-known names of formerly independent companies: Knopf, Viking, Simon & Schuster, etc. But they are part of a group, and frequently, if a manuscript is declined by one of these companies, it has in effect been declined by every other publisher in the corporation.

The effect of this consolidation is not just that there are fewer places to submit a manuscript but also that the money people who control these corporations tend to think of books as merely a product to be sold. I don't mean the editors, most of whom are still as passionate about books as they always were. I'm talking about the heads of multi-national conglomerates and the effect of their bottom-line influence. Formerly, a manuscript went to an editorial board. If the editors felt a passion for it, the book was accepted. But now many editorial boards don't buy anything until the marketing department (a new force in publishing) takes a look, and the marketing department will ask the following question: "What's the author's platform?"

In the context of a novel, one of the things "platform" refers to is the non-fiction subject of the plot. This concept baffles some authors. They wrote a novel. How can it have a non-fiction subject? I remember an unpublished writer talking to me about his hero, who likes to drive cars and gets jilted by his girl friend. "She has an affair with his rival," the young writer explained, "so the hero decides to get revenge by . . ." The object of the conversation was for the author to pretend I was a marketer in a publishing house. His purpose was to convince me to accept the manuscript.

But I needed to tell him to stop. "You're giving me the plot," I said. "If I'm a marketer, I don't want to hear the plot. Journalists don't want to hear the plot. Radio and TV interviewers don't want to hear it. Their audiences don't want to hear it. Summarized plot is boring. That's why we read the book, to get the fully dramatized story. But summarizing the plot isn't going to make readers buy it."

"Then let me tell you about the hero's background."

"Same problem," I said.

"He likes to drive cars. That's all he ever wanted to do since he was a kid."

"But who's the book intended for? Any special type of reader? Someone who might have an interest in the book's subject. You still haven't told me what the subject is."

The young writer stared at me in exasperation and finally said, "Would it help if I told you he's a NASCAR driver?"

"This book's about NASCAR?" I asked in surprise.

"Yeah, I love going to the races. I know the drivers. They let me hang around with the crew in the pits."

"Why didn't you say so in the first place?"

"I guess I was too focused on the characters and the plot."

"Would the drivers give you publicity quotes for the book?"

"Sure."

"Could bookstores sell your novel at the races?"

"Absolutely."

"Could you arrange to have an ad for your book on one of the cars?"

"No problem."

"You've got a platform."

In case you're not aware, NASCAR is the most popular sporting event in the United States (assuming that racing cars is a sport). Fans buy everything associated with it. All a marketer needs to hear is, "This is a fast-paced novel about life on the NASCAR circuit. It's about a rivalry between two drivers for the woman they love. There are plenty of background details about the races. The novelist can get blurbs from famous drivers. He's prepared to sign books at the events. He has plenty of inside stories to tell the media."

The marketer now has enough information to recommend offering a contract for the manuscript. He doesn't actually need to read the book. That's the editor's job. All he cares about is whether there's an audience for the non-fiction subject of the story and whether there's a way to market the book to those readers. In short, the book has a platform. (Some of these promotional ideas were actually part of the campaign for Brad Meltzer's bestselling novel, *The Book of Fate*. Because its first chapter features a NASCAR race, an ad for the book was put on a car in a race at Richmond,

Virginia. A book sponsor was considered so unusual that the ad received a close-up on national television. A professional driver then interviewed Brad for NASCAR's website.)

In today's publishing environment, a first-time novelist has trouble getting a contract if the book doesn't have a promotable non-fiction subject. My heart aches when a writer comes to me and says something like, "I just finished a noir private-eye novel set in Chicago." A noir private-eye novel is by definition a subgenre. Some readers are addicted to that type of book, but not enough to pique the interest of a major marketing department. Sure, maybe some Chicago readers might also buy the book, provided there are plenty of accurate local details. But, again, those readers wouldn't be enough to merit a contract. Marketers need a unique element in the novel that will appeal to an identifiable group of book buyers and that will also suggest ways to make that group aware of the book, and that element must be something that can be discussed apart from the details of the plot.

Christine Goff's mysteries are excellent examples of what I mean. An avid birdwatcher, one of more than forty million in the United States, she had the inspiration to write a series of novels about what she loves. Her titles clearly identify her topic: *A Rant of Ravens*, for instance, and *Death of a Songbird*. These mysteries describe such important subjects as massive die-offs of birds and the implications for the planet. In *Death Shoots a Birdie*, Christine begins with the murder of a keynote speaker at a birding convention and ends with a race to save a bird species on the edge of extinction. Strictly speaking, that last sentence is about plot, but I included it because it also illustrates how Christine's books are promoted. She gives talks at numerous well-attended birding conventions. She arranges for her books to be sold there. She contributes articles to major birding websites. A book with a birding topic that occurs at a birding convention is almost sure to attract attention in that community. As a bonus, the cover of *Death Shoots a Birdie* takes advantage of the title's allusion to golfing and shows a bird on a golf course, standing next to a golf ball that looks like an egg in a nest. That allows the book, which involves the development of a golf course, to be cross-promoted to golfers as well as birders.

I'm not suggesting that Christine started the series with any of these marketing possibilities in mind. She began with a passion for her subject, and as her birdwatcher's mystery series evolved, she found a way to interact with readers. Any novel written to conform to a preconceived marketing plan is almost certain to seem lifeless and cynical. But after you've written the best novel you can, don't you want readers to buy the book and appreciate the story you worked so hard to create? Doesn't it make sense for you to step back from your honestly written novel and consider various aspects of it that you can use to attract book buyers?

"That's not my job," you say. "I'll let the publicity department invent ways to sell the book." The problem is that, if you're a first-time novelist, you're not going to get the full attention of the publicity department. In fact, publicity departments are so over-worked and understaffed that sometimes even bestselling authors don't get full attention. When an author comes to them with a fresh, interesting, useful way to attract readers, they're so grateful that they'll give you far more attention than they would to an author who takes them for granted.

That assumes you have a contract, and if you don't have a marketing plan when you submit your book, if you don't identify your "platform," the chances are that the publisher won't show interest. Indeed, the agents you approach probably won't show interest, either. The days of submitting a query letter in which all you do is introduce yourself and provide a plot summary are over. You need to tell the agent or the editor the kind of book you've written, why you think there's a market for it, and how the book can be promoted.

Here's an example of how the process works. When I started my novel *Creepers*, it was in response to a newspaper article whose topic fascinated me: urban explorers. One of their nicknames is "creepers," and although I didn't know anything about them before I read the article, I sure wanted to know more afterward.

Urban explorers are history and architecture enthusiasts who infiltrate old buildings that have been sealed and abandoned for decades. Because old buildings are dangerous, the explorers often wear hardhats, construction-worker boots, equipment belts, and noxious-gas detectors. The activity is illegal (punishable by serious fines and jail terms), so the explorers need to muster all their cleverness to avoid being caught. They have strict ethics: take nothing but photographs; leave nothing but footprints. Unexpectedly, many abandoned buildings still have the original furniture—old sofas, chairs, newspapers, vintage telephones and televisions, etc. Entering those buildings can feel like stepping into the past.

I asked myself, "Who hasn't wanted to explore an old building? It's almost a universal urge." I remembered several old buildings that I'd explored as a child. As my novelist's imagination began to suggest a plot, I realized that I needed to do more research, so I Googled "urban explorers," and to my surprise, I got a quarter of a million hits. Urban explorers, I discovered, exist all around the world. Australia, Russia, Germany, Italy, France, England: the underground culture of creepers is everywhere. I couldn't restrain my enthusiasm as I made notes and then spent the next six months letting my imagination roam the eerie, cobwebbed corridors of an abandoned building I called the Paragon Hotel.

As you're aware, that's how novels get written. An idea grabs you, and you let it take you. But after the manuscript was completed, another idea suddenly grabbed me, and that's when the marketing part of my imagination took over. Maybe you didn't see the importance of one of the statements in the previous paragraph. I'll say it again. I Googled "urban explorers" and got a quarter of a million hits. Holy . . . ! The first time I noticed this, my primary reaction was, "Plenty of research materials." But the second time, I thought, "Look at all these websites. It's logical to assume there are plenty of urban explorers associated with each site. If the publisher sends copies of the book to these sites, if the sites think I treated their activity fairly, maybe they'll review the book and spread the word about it. The potential readership is huge."

Then I thought, "The Paragon Hotel is set in Asbury Park, New Jersey, which is one of the saddest cities in the United States—once a crown jewel resort on the eastern seaboard before a hurricane, a fire, and a riot made it a near ruin. Perhaps the publisher can send copies of the book to websites that specialize in tragic aspects of New Jersey. Maybe those sites will spread the word also. Not as big a market as urban exploration. Still, it's another approach."

Then I thought, "But *Creepers* is a thriller with a moody tone that feels like a horror novel. A mixed genre. Perhaps I can get in touch with Internet horror sites and see if they're interested in my mixed-genre experiment." Eventually, I crossed paths with Nanci Kalanta, who owns www.horrorworld.org. She liked the book enough that she promoted it and let other horror sites know about it. She arranged for contests in which visitors to the various sites had a chance to win signed copies of the novel. She featured a BE A CREEPER game that showed a hotel lobby and told the viewer to find the way to a treasure. Two choices were offered: go to the right or the left. If you clicked the wrong button, you faced a white rat with pink eyes and the word EEEK coming from its mouth. The effect was amusing.

So you went back to the lobby and tried the other way, only to face the choice of going up or down. The latter led to a raging stream. Through various stages, you overcame obstacles until you finally entered the hotel's penthouse, where you found the treasure. And what was that? The chance to read the afterword to *Creepers* and learn about urban exploration. But if you wanted to win valuable prizes, you could enter a contest, which required you to reply to questions, the answers to which were available at my website.

All this was done in a humorous way and is an example of a concept called "viral marketing." The term has nothing to do with computer viruses, as it might suggest, but instead refers to what Seth Godin proposed in his landmark book, *Launching the Ideavirus*: that ideas can multiply and travel with the speed of a viral contagion if they are presented in an intriguing enough way. A good example is a promotional tactic by the Starbucks coffee shop chain. Starbucks hired a handful of representatives to glue Starbucks' coffee containers to the top of their cars. Each container looked as if it had been forgotten on the car's roof after the driver put it there to free his or her hands to pull out car keys and open the door. The representatives drove at random through major America cities. When they stopped at red lights, pedestrians pointed in alarm, trying to warn the driver about the precious Starbucks' coffee container forgotten on the roof. The driver got out, pretended to be surprised by the container, then grinned, and handed out coupons for free Starbucks coffee. This inexpensive campaign was so clever that it caught the attention of the media, which widely reported it, including on national television. I, in turn, thought it was so clever that I'm telling you about it. I suspect that you'll tell someone else. The way something is promoted becomes so interesting that people pass it around like gossip. That's viral marketing.

For *Creepers*, I wanted an object that would serve as a prize for the contests and as a gift to book stores and the publisher's sales representatives, something associated with the subject of the novel, something that would serve as a symbol for it. The inspiration for this goes back to . . . can you guess? . . . Jacqueline Susann. The cover of her 1969 novel, *The Love Machine*, featured an Egyptian cross known as an ankh—it has a loop at the top and symbolizes life. Jackie had numerous ankhs designed as promotional gifts: rings, bracelet charms, earrings, etc. The symbol appeared on her stationary. But the most impressive ankhs took the form of gold pendants, for each of which she paid $83, at a time when $83 was a lot of money. Jackie gave these to influential people with whom she worked. One evening, while having dinner with my agent, Jane Dystel, I explained my admiration for Jackie's marketing abilities. Jane smiled and lifted something that hung from her neck. A gold ankh pendant. It turns out that Jane's father, Oscar Dystel, was the president of Bantam Books for thirty years, during which time he published Jackie's paperbacks. Jackie gave him one of the ankhs, which he kept framed on a wall in his office until he gave it to Jane after he retired. I can't think of a more vivid example of how a carefully chosen promotional gift can have a long-lasting impact.

The gift for *Creepers* wasn't as classy and expensive as that ankh, but it did make people smile: the *Creepers* survival kit. This was a first-aid kit in a small blue nylon pouch with a sturdy zipper. The pouch contained band-aids, antiseptic wipes, aspirins, and cough drops. It was imprinted with my name, the title of the book, and the publisher's name. Attached to it on a sturdy key ring was a quality LED light imprinted with the same information. This useful, distinctive gift generated a lot of viral-marketing conversation. Each unit cost around $3.50 and is typical of similar items that you can find by doing an Internet search for "printable promotions."

Several websites can help stimulate your imagination about viral marketing: www.jakonrath.com, www.barryeisler.com, and www.mjrose.com, for example. These sites belong to gifted novelists who are also skilled marketers, and each provides a section on that topic. They also provide links to other sites that discuss book promotion.

As you educate yourself, you'll discover all kinds of easy things you can do. Make sure that your website has a way for readers to send you email messages. Answer every message. Many authors don't, thus disappointing readers instead of ingratiating them. Ask your website designer to provide a way to collect the email address of every message sent to you. That enables you to send news releases, but make clear on your website that anyone who contacts you will receive occasional mass emails from you. Otherwise, you'll be considered a spammer. Adjust your email signature so that every message you send has an automatic note at the end, mentioning your new book, the publisher, and a statement that summarizes the tone and theme of the work. For *Creepers*, I used "The darkest secrets live in places you're not supposed to be." Three lines of information are sufficient.

Order postcards and business cards that show the book's cover and display promotional information on the back. On the Internet, many printing companies offer amazingly low rates for these items. Carry the cards with you and hand them out when the situation is appropriate. Make sure they indicate your website address and any website devoted to your book (www.the paragonhotel.com was the *Creepers* website, for example). Buy ads in magazines (print and Internet) that specialize in your type of fiction. Also, buy ads in magazines devoted to the non–fiction subject of your novel. The cost of reaching this targeted readership is minimal compared to an advertisement in a national newspaper and might even achieve equal results. Teach yourself to make podcasts and videocasts. Create a presence on MySpace, YouTube, and similar Internet sites. The geometric progression of ideas and media devices yet to be invented excites me. I suspect the use of these opportunities in the future, especially electronic ones, will be as varied as the characters and plots of novels yet unwritten.

Earlier, I said that book tours aren't as effective as they used to be, but that doesn't mean they can't be productive if you approach them from an innovative perspective. The traditional fifteen–city tour is enormously expensive: air fare, hotel rooms, meals, escorts who drive authors to stores and media interviews, etc. Many escorts charge more than $300 a day. A tour to fifteen cities can cost over $15,000, which is why most publishers finance tours only for mega-selling authors.

But what if you showed your publisher that you could arrange a tour for a considerably low cost? Among enterprising authors, it's become a challenge to see who can manage the lowest priced, most dramatic tour. First, identify the stores whose specialty fits the type of book you've written. This is easily done by using the Internet to study the list of stores at sites such as www.bookweb.org/members/. *Creepers* was a mixture of thriller and horror, so I made a list of the appropriate stores and looked for clusters in various areas. I made appointments at those stores, then flew to those areas, rented a car, and used an Internet-acquired map or a GPS receiver to find my way to all the locations (thus eliminating the cost of an escort). Often, I drove from city to city (thus eliminating the cost of an airline ticket). At one point, I flew to Cincinnati, Ohio, rented a car, and visited stores all across that state. Why Ohio? Because it has a lot of stores that report to the *USA Today* bestseller list (every Thursday, the names of the stores are mentioned at the bottom of the list). I stayed in the cheapest motels imaginable and ate take-out sandwiches while I drove. I posted frequent reports at various Internet sites, detailing my adventures, complete with photographs of weird things I saw en route and motels that looked like they were inspired by Alfred Hitchcock's *Psycho*. These reports generated comments and thus became a form of viral marketing. In the end, I traveled to ten states, drove five thousand miles, visited fifty stores, and was able to do it for $5,000. A dollar a mile. My publisher was happy to pay.

But my experiment was nothing compared to J.A. Konrath's goal of visiting every store in the United States. Among other things, he writes crime novels that are a unique blend of terror and humor. His main character is a female homicide detective, Jackie Daniels. Her name echoes that of the whiskey manufacturer Jack Daniels. Appropriately, each novel is titled after an alcoholic beverage, *Rusty Nail*, for example, or *Dirty Martini*. Instead of business cards, he hands out beverage coasters printed with information about his books. He puts a magnetically attached strip on each side of his car, displaying the cover of his latest work. To date, he's visited almost one thousand stores. He hopes to get in the *Guinness Book of Records*. His quest generated a lot of talk, as did Barry Eisler's epical 11,000-mile drive back and forth across the United States to promote his John Rain novel, *The Last Assassin*. That's viral marketing.

For a beginning author, however, the main purpose of a book tour isn't to sell books. Rather, your goal is to meet the store owners and establish a long-term relationship. I once did a two-hour signing in a major Los Angeles bookstore during a power blackout. Not one customer was in the store. But the clerks were there and in particular the manager, with whom I chatted at length. I asked questions about the manager's perception of the book business and learned a great deal. I explained my background and why I became a writer. We established sufficient rapport that, when I left, the manager promised to promote my books whenever possible. Especially for a new writer, this sort of contact is invaluable. With luck and effort, the sales will come later. For now, your purpose is to introduce yourself and hope to be remembered when your next book comes out.

Arnold Schwarzenegger may seem an unusual person to mention in this context, but I never forgot something he once said in an interview: that he expected to spend as much time promoting a film as he did acting in it. The average length of a film shoot is three months, and I believe an ambitious author should plan to spend three months promoting a novel, although not necessarily in one chunk of time. Organizing a viral marketing campaign can be time consuming, for instance, as can choosing and ordering promotional materials, not to mention signing your books at events devoted to the non-fiction subject of your novel.

In an ideal world, your publisher will do a lot of the promotional work for you, but that's not a certainty, especially if you're a beginning author. You need to assume control of your career and come up with your own inventive methods of letting readers know about your fiction. Bring to promotion the same enthusiasm and creative energy you bring to your writing. A couple of years ago, I spoke with a well-known novelist whose sales were in decline. His frustration was obvious when he asked me what I thought he could do to increase his numbers. I explained the publicity lessons I'd learned. He looked at me in shock. "I'm an author. I don't do that stuff," he said. His sales are now even lower.

In contrast, I think of those first-time novelists determined enough to succeed that they spend their entire advances on ways to promote their work. I also think of Jackie Susann, who contracted breast cancer in the early 1960s. After a mastectomy, she tirelessly pursued her career, publicizing her books at every opportunity. The cancer returned in 1973. Her big black wigs, it turned out, were necessary because underneath them she was bald from chemotherapy. The end came a year later, but until she went to the hospital for the final time, she never stopped promoting.

Questions I'm Often Asked

E very class should have a question-and-answer session.

Q: *What qualities do you think a fiction writer needs in order to have a career?*
A: There's an old joke about a new convict in prison. A seasoned inmate tries to show the new guy how the place is run. During lunch in the prison's mess hall, a grizzled prisoner jumps up and yells, "Twenty-six!" The rest of the inmates bust a gut laughing. A prisoner with a scar on his face leaps up and yells, "Forty-two!" Ha, ha! Guffaws all around. A prisoner with tattoos shouts, "Seventy-five!" Inmates laugh so hard they roll on the floor.

"What's going on?" the new convict asks his guide.

The old man explains, "Most of us have been in here so long we've run out of fresh jokes, so we gave numbers to the jokes we memorized, and to save time, we just yell the numbers."

The new guy thinks about this. Wanting to be popular, he springs to his feet and yells, "Eleven!" Deadly silence. All the inmates look at him blankly. Red faced with embarrassment, he sinks to his chair and says to his guide, "I don't understand. Everybody else yells a number and gets laughs. But when *I* yell a number, all they do is stare at me."

"Well," says his guide, "some people just don't know how to tell a joke."

Exactly. And some people just don't know how to tell a story. They're like a would-be musician who is tone deaf. Or a failed dancer with no sense of rhythm. Unless you have an ability to hold someone's attention, unless you have a sense of pace and drama (what movie executives annoyingly call the "beats" of a story), it won't matter how much craft you learn; you'll never be a success as a fiction writer. This ability cannot be taught. You're born with it.

But if you have that gift, knowledge of craft will make all the difference. Technique *can* be learned, although as I've emphasized you don't want to imitate someone else's technique. Instead, you want to understand the principles of viewpoint, structure, description, dialogue, and so on, to produce something new.

After storytelling skill and technical ability, the next quality you need is determination. I've known many writers with far better imagination and verbal talent than I have. But they never had a career because they didn't want it badly enough. They didn't do what was necessary, which was to plant their butts on their chairs and do the work. Writers write. They don't talk about writing. They don't promise themselves that, one day when inspiration strikes, they'll start putting words on a page. They do it.

When Stirling Silliphant wrote for *Route 66*, he did almost three-quarters of that show's 116 hour-long episodes. The program was filmed at various American locations, a new city every week, so he had to keep a month ahead of the production team. He would arrive in Phoenix, for example, introduce himself to the local CBS affiliate (CBS broadcast the show), get a tour of the city, then sequester himself in a hotel room, and write the script for that city. Four days later, he was on the road again. Simultaneously, he also wrote for (and was the story consultant for) the prestigious police drama *Naked City*. In a pre-computer society, there was a Hollywood joke that went like this.

Question: How on earth can Stirling Silliphant write so fast?

Answer: He has an electric typewriter.

In the late 1980s, I visited Stirling after his wisdom teeth were extracted. The procedure occurred at eight in the morning. My visit was at noon. I found him pounding away at a keyboard. His cheeks were swollen and packed with cotton batting. He looked like a squirrel with nuts in its mouth. But he was hitting those keys. For a half hour, he took time off to have a cup of tea with me. I suspect that he wouldn't have taken the break if I weren't there. Then I was out the door, and he was back to work.

Stephen King once told me about his vasectomy. The surgical procedure occurred in the morning. His physician advised him to go easy for the rest of the day. Instead, Steve went to work as soon as he got home. Only when he looked down and realized that he was sitting in a pool of blood and that his testicles were swollen did he finally quit.

From 1970 to 1986, I combined writing with my professorial duties at the University of Iowa. Determined to do the job I was paid for, I scrupulously conducted classes that had as many as two hundred students. I prepared for the next day's classes, met with students, graded papers, and participated in committee meetings. The university got good value. But in order to do that and to create fiction, I worked seven days a week. A typical day began at five in the morning when I started to write. At eight I showered and went to school. I put in my eight hours, eating a sandwich during noon hour while squeezing in a little writing time. Around four, I went to the gym for a half-hour run. I came home, spent time with my family, ate dinner, prepared for the next day's classes, and went to sleep around eleven. The next day I was up at five, writing. Weekends, I took it slightly easy and wrote only until early afternoon. That's a brutal schedule. I don't know how I kept at it so long, but I never saw it as a hardship. I did it because I wanted to. Because teaching was my love and writing was my passion. It was a wonderful time. Then one day I ran out of energy and knew that I needed to make a commitment to academia or to writing fiction, not to both. There was never any doubt it would be writing.

You also need to feel comfortable being alone. Apart from being a monk, a lighthouse keeper, or a forest-fire spotter, I can't think of a more solitary profession than being a writer. I'm an only child. I spent most of my youth by myself. I don't mind being alone. Sometimes I crave it. In contrast, I know some would-be writers who can't make themselves sit still for long. They need companionship. They need social reinforcement. After ten minutes of writing, they suddenly reach for the phone because ten minutes is too long a time not to have talked with someone. For a writer, this is a fatal flaw. You should think of the telephone as your enemy, not your friend. You should dread interruptions, not hope for them.

One way people who need people try to solve this problem is by choosing a writing partner. With exceptions such as Douglas Preston and Lincoln Child, this arrangement usually results in a lot of talk and nothing on the page, in broken friendships rather than readable prose, but if you're determined to try writing with someone, make sure you have a lawyer-approved signed agreement that stipulates the amount of work each person is expected to do and the percentage of income to which each is entitled. That way, you're protected if the two of you write a publishable book but can no longer tolerate each other.

The final thing you need is luck. Even if you're skilled and determined, the novels you write might never catch an editor's attention. Or if an editor likes your work, book buyers might not. From a career point of view, a novel can be beautifully written but still not speak to its culture. Sometimes it happens in the reverse. Arguably, the worst-written classic American novel is Theodore Dreiser's *Sister Carrie*. Its theme is pessimistic determinism, that fate and the environment will lead us to a bad end. Not exactly the stuff of best-sellers. The prose is awful: "Here comes the moths." "It was a truly swell saloon." But the trials of its heroine spoke so directly to readers that the book became part of American culture.

When John Grisham's *The Firm* was published, I happened to be in an airport bookstore as copies of the book were put on display. The cover showed a businessman in a tightlooking suit, holding a briefcase, while a puppeteer's strings controlled his movement. Business traveler after business traveler stopped and stared at that cover, then bought the book. *They* were the person on that cover. *They* were the hero who sold his soul to a corporation, controlled by "strings." They couldn't resist buying it.

Consider the following widely different novels: Joseph Heller's *Catch-22*. Mario Puzo's *The Godfather*. Peter Benchley's *Jaws*. Heller's is a stylistic masterpiece. Puzo's has basic professional prose. Benchley's has serious structural problems (he keeps cutting away from the shark to deal with the hero's boring domestic problems). Nonetheless, these books and Grisham's have one thing in common. The stories they told spoke to book buyers in powerful mysterious ways that cannot be predicted. The authors had the good fortune to care about things that book buyers happened to care about. This happens only about a hundred times each year. But in the case of the books I just mentioned, they not only mirrored our culture—they contributed to it. And *that's* so rare, it happens maybe only a couple of times a decade.

You can't control the lucky coincidence in which the culture's interests happen to match your book's subject. All you can do is apply yourself and write the best book you can. After that, it's in the hands of fate.

Q: *Do you think it's important to have a structured day?*
A: For me, that's absolutely necessary. I try to get to work by eight or eight-thirty. I take a break in the middle of the day to play tennis. I eat something and then get back to work, finishing around five or five-thirty. I no longer work on weekends. After my son died from cancer in 1987, my energy level was never the same. I still get a lot done (five pages a day), but I find a few days of rest to be good for my imagination.

Some writers are ruthless in their adherence to a schedule. A famous example is Georges Simenon, the French mystery writer and creator of Inspector Maigret. Incredibly prolific, Simenon was so committed to a schedule that, if he took a walk at a certain time on the first day of working on a book, he would walk at that exact same time for the remainder of the days he worked on that book. Day after day, he always followed the same route, never varying it.

This might seem like needless obsession. But actually there's a logic to it. When you're working on a long project, it's possible that sticking to a schedule and not allowing your imagination to be distracted by something new gives your subconscious the room to concentrate solely on your story. A lot of creative work happens when we're away from the desk. Often we don't realize it, but as we drive to a grocery store or we brush our teeth, in those mundane tasks that we do without thinking, our imagination is building strength and making connections. If we're bombarded with new stimuli when we're not at our desk, the subconscious is too busy adjusting to concentrate on the work at hand.

On a larger level, I worry that a life-changing event will occur when I'm halfway through a book, something so overwhelming (it can be positive as much as negative) that it makes me feel detached from the book I'm writing. Sometimes a powerfully good or bad thing happens to a writer, preventing him or her from returning to the mood of a novel. A defined schedule can help protect against that creative danger so that, even if something overwhelming does happen to you, the habit of your schedule will protect the book.

Don't use my schedule as a model. Everybody's different. I'm a day person, but you might be a night person. There was a time when Donald E. Westlake didn't start working until after the late television news. Then he wrote until dawn and went to sleep. Some writers find that their best work comes in the afternoon. Some aren't able to write for more than three hours at a stretch. Figure out what's best for you. Maybe you're a single mother with an office job. You have all kinds of demands on your time. But if you're determined, you'll find an hour a day that's yours and write what you can during that period. The important thing is, stick to whatever schedule you lay out for yourself.

Q: *Do you recommend writers programs at universities?*
A: There are many first-class writers programs around the country: the famous Writers Workshop at the University of Iowa, for example. I mention it first because I know it well, having had an office on the

floor below it when I taught in the English department at that university. Stanford has a good one. So do Johns Hopkins and the State University of New York at Buffalo and Binghamton. The University of Arizona also comes to mind. There are plenty of others. Write to various programs and ask to be sent information. Get a list of the faculty. Read what they've written. Are you enthusiastic enough about their prose to want to work with those authors?

Along with your application, you send samples of your work. A faculty committee reviews your submission and decides whether to admit you. If you're accepted, you join other apprentice writers in classes devoted to discussing your work and that of your classmates while a faculty member officiates. You have one-on-one meetings with your instructor. You're also expected to take literature classes.

The advantage of this method is that you're among other creative people in an environment that encourages you to write. You've got a qualified reader (your instructor), and if the students reading your work aren't yet qualified, at least they're struggling with the same problems that you are, so you're all working toward a common goal.

A disadvantage is that, with exceptions, writers programs don't like to provide instruction in technique. Their assumption is that you should be encouraged to explore, to develop your own ways of expression. They worry that if you take classes in technique, you'll do things the way other writers have and become imitative, a legitimate concern. But there's a difference between pointing out common technical mistakes and encouraging an apprentice writer to use a certain method. In this book, much of my advice has been negative: "Don't do this, don't do that." It comes after painful years of having discovered that some approaches are likely not to be effective. I don't see the harm in having a few classes about viewpoint, structure, and dialogue. For the most part, though, you won't get that kind of guidance at a writers program. You'll be expected to discover those things on your own and possibly waste time.

Another problem about writers' programs is that, with exceptions, they tend to encourage fiction that is consciously literary. It doesn't matter how serious you are about reinventing a genre, about bringing a new perspective to commercial writing; you won't fit in. If, to apply to a program, you submit a first-rate science fiction story or, heaven forbid, a horror story, you'll be rejected automatically. One science-fiction writer I know, a multiple prize winner, among the best and most creative in his field, Joe Haldeman (*The Forever War*), somehow squeezed his science-fiction ambitions past the application committee at a leading writers program and still can't get over how badly he was treated when they discovered his intentions.

So do I recommend them? Yes and no. For a certain kind of writer, they can be a powerfully positive experience. If you want to try writing stories for *The New Yorker*, you'll feel at home. Plus, the degree you earn might get you a day job teaching creative writing. But if you want to reinvent the techno-thriller (something that needs to be done), traditional writers programs won't help you, not that you'd ever be accepted if you were honest about what you wanted to write. A few schools do encourage genre writing, however, particularly Seton Hill University in Pennsylvania, which offers a master's program in that category.

Each year, there are dozens of weekend writing workshops across the country. These are usually advertised in *Writer's Digest* and *The Writer* magazines (readily available at large magazine counters). Choose a weekend conference near you, and give it a try. You don't need to submit a story to get in. All you need to do is pay a fee. Published authors give seminars every hour. The topics vary. Genres are treated with the same respect as mainstream fiction. The goal is to help you get published. Sometimes agents and editors show up. It's a good way to make contacts and gain experience. In the same vein, the Horror Writers Association, the Mystery Writers of America, the Western Writers of America, the Romance Writers of America, and the International Thriller Writers organization are helpful, with newsletters, websites, and conferences.

Q: *Do you think every writer should use a word-processing program on a computer?*

A: For me, a computer is helpful because I can easily revise. In the old days, when I used a typewriter, even the simplest change meant that I needed to retype a page. The wasted time and the stress on my fingers made me think hard before revising. Now, with a computer (I've worn out four of them), I make changes eagerly.

But some writers don't like computers. A friend, Justin Scott (*The Shipkiller*), found the glowing screen so oppressive that he went back to his typewriter. Harlan Ellison (more about him later) finds computers so damaging to creativity that he keeps a ready supply of the brand of typewriter he prefers so he never runs out of spare parts. In my own case, I'm certain that staring at a screen all day has weakened my eyes. I take care to leave my desk every hour and stare at the horizon. Nonetheless, at the end of a work day, I occasionally have a computer-generated headache.

Some writers type. Some, like John Barth, use a pad and a pencil and then transfer their day's work to a computer. Whatever it takes. But if you do use a computer, make sure that you transfer your work to a jump drive or CD at the end of each session and that you take that device to another room. That way, if something happens to your computer (it's stolen or it spontaneously combusts), you still have a copy of your work. For the same reason, I recommend printing your work at the end of each session and taking the pages to another room. A further reason for printing your work is that it gives you a chance to read it under conditions that are different from staring at a computer screen. The change in perspective helps you notice mistakes.

Ever since I learned that Ralph Ellison's follow-up novel to *Invisible Man* was destroyed in a fire, I've had a phobia about leaving manuscripts unprotected. Make copies. Store them away from your computer. Even experienced writers can forget this elementary principle. Edward T. Hall, a social anthropologist and one of the few geniuses I've been privileged to meet (he pioneered the study of personal space and of body language; read *The Hidden Dimension* and *The Silent Language*) once told me that his office was burglarized. Not only was his computer stolen, but his backup disc and the printout of his manuscript, both of which he had left next to his computer, were also missing. A year's work was lost. Keep your memory device, your printout, and your computer separated.

Also, take your backup device and use it in another computer to make certain that the device isn't defective and that your computer has in fact been copying files onto it. Imagine your heartache if theft or fire leave you with only your memory device. Proud that you remembered to make one, you install it on another computer and discover . . . nothing.

Finally, avoid the following when using a word-processing program to format your manuscript:

1) Do not justify your right-hand margin, using an au-to-ma-tic hy-phen func-tion. This is cruel to your copyeditor. Before your manuscript goes to the printer, the copyeditor will need to do the extra work of removing all the hyphens that don't normally occur in the way certain words are spelled.

Some computer programs justify the right-hand margin by altering the spaces between words rather than arbitrarily hyphen-ating. If you absolutely feel the need to have that neat right-hand margin, it's permissible to use the space-altering function, but I'm traditional enough to feel that the ragged right edge looks more like a manuscript, and some editors feel the same way.

2) Do not use the "widows and orphans" function. This function looks for pages that end with the start of a paragraph (an orphan) or else pages that begin with the end of a paragraph (a widow). The function removes these orphans and widows by dropping the bottom line of one page and adding it to the top of the next one. In the process, it creates an empty double space at the bottom of the page from which the line was moved. The theory is that widows and orphans look awkward, but I never heard an agent or an editor complain about them, and in my opinion, this quest for neatness creates its own problems. Those empty double spaces at the bottom can be distracting after a while, making pages look skimpy. Moreover,

a lot of pages will now end with complete paragraphs, and that is a liability when you're trying to use every device you can think of to encourage an agent or an editor to turn the pages. In a passage that might not be your most interesting, a sentence that carries from one page to the next might be your only hope of getting someone to keep reading, whereas a lot of pages that end with full stops might encourage a not-yet-impressed reader to do just that: stop.

Q: *With so much rereading and revising, how do you keep from losing objectivity about a manuscript?*

A: If you use a computer, I already mentioned the value of reading a passage on the computer screen and then reading that passage on paper. The difference in format will help you find basic mistakes. Similarly, change the fonts on your printer from time to time. If you're accustomed to Courier Old, as I am, print out a version of the manuscript in Times New Roman. The manuscript will take on a new reality. If you compose first in longhand, you already know how different and fresh your fiction becomes when you read a typed version.

I find it helpful to revise my manuscripts at various places. I have two tables in my office. I often switch back and forth. Somehow, the manuscript becomes different in a new locale. If, as I did years ago, you write in what amounts to a closet, try revising at the kitchen table (when nobody's around) rather than at your desk. Or at the chair where you normally watch television. Or on a back porch. Or at a library. The change will give you a new perspective.

The most important tactic I use in order to see a familiar manuscript in a new constructive way is to imagine someone such as Stirling Silliphant or Philip Klass leaning over my shoulder, commenting on the work. "Did you really mean to say it that way, David? Is that passage clear enough? Don't you think this paragraph can use a little more sense detail? How about some extra drama here?" Often it's my agent or my editor I imagine leaning over my shoulder. Whoever, it must be someone whose opinion I respect and whose critical principles I understand. I find this role-playing to be especially useful in the final stages of a book.

Q: *Do you have any advice about choosing names for characters?*

A: Many authors have an almost mystical attachment to the names they give characters. I once had a heated discussion with a fellow writer who insisted that "Decker" was better than "Becker." The artist hero of my novel, *Burnt Sienna*, was originally called Kincaid, but then I discovered there was an actual artist with that name, although he spelled it differently. Concerned about legal liabilities (always something to bear in mind), I changed Kincaid to Malone. For about a week, I felt intense loss. Now I have trouble recalling the original name. Decker, Kincaid, Malone. Basically, these names are abstractions, and viewing them as such helps me detect annoying patterns. At the start of a novel, I make a list of characters' names to ensure that each begins with a different letter of the alphabet, thus preventing a repetition of Anna, Albert, and Aaron. The list also helps me to avoid names with similar endings: Harry, Bobby, and Tommy. Note that those names have the same syllables, as do Corrigan, Matheson, and Farraday, names that would be rhythmically wearying if all three were in the same story. I try to vary all of these elements. I also try to avoid names with "s" in them. Imagine that your book is being recorded. Persistent "Susan said"'s will not make your audio-book narrator happy.

Q: *How many drafts do you write?*

A: If we interpret "draft" in a large sense, I write three. In my first draft, I try to write quickly, to go with the flow. I reread the previous day's pages at the start of the new work day. I bring myself up to speed in the narrative. I edit for grammar and clarity. But I keep moving. I don't want to stifle the story. If I have doubts about whether to put something in, I err on the side of excess and include it.

In my second draft, I look at the shapeless mess I've created. I trim and focus, often eliminating one-third of the manuscript, clarifying the book's structure.

But then I reread this second draft and realize that I've been too stringent, that I've cut too much and excised the life from the narrative. In my third draft, I put material back in and give the narrative some breathing room. It's this draft that I send to my agent and my editor.

For you, this process might work in the opposite way. Perhaps your first drafts are meager. Perhaps you amplify in your second draft and cut to an acceptable version in the third.

Remember to save each draft. Few things are more frustrating than to look at your final draft and decide that the first draft or the second had a better version of a given chapter. But when you search for that previous version, you're sickened to discover that, in an excess of confidence about your final draft, you threw those other drafts away. You worked hard on those other drafts. Why be eager to get rid of them? Save everything.

Q: *Is it okay to throw drafts out after the book has been published?*
A: No. Keep your various drafts forever. Store them in a big box along with your research materials (photos, maps, magazine arti-cles, and the like). Put your written conversation with yourself in the same box, along with all correspondence that you had with your agent and editor. Basically, you're creating an archive. Down the road, you might have occasion to refer to these materials if you need to refresh your memory about the creative process. Maybe you're writing an introduction for an edition twenty years later. Or maybe somebody wants to write an article or a book about you. Don't reduce the possibilities by failing to save the history of your work.

Keep a separate file for all reviews and publicity materials. You can't count on your publisher to do this. Over the years I've had numerous reprints of my novels, and in each case, the new publisher always asks me for copies of reviews and anything else that will help them package and promote the book. If I hadn't saved everything, we'd be starting from scratch and wasting a lot of time.

Keep a detailed bibliography of everything you publish: novels, short stories, book reviews, magazine articles, introductions to work by others, foreign editions, letters to newspapers, whatever.

If you wrote it and it appeared in print, no matter how short and trivial-seeming, make a note of it. In your bibliography, also include interviews you gave and newspaper articles about you. Keep a copy of everything noted in the bibliography. The goal is to have a record of your career. At the end of each year, I send a box of copies of these materials to the Special Collections Department at the University of Iowa's library. I retain the various stages of my manuscripts in case I need to refer to them later, as I did in 1994 when I decided to publish an alternate draft of my 1979 novel, *The Totem*. Otherwise, copies of everything I've written are at a separate safe location.

Q: *Anything else about the business of writing?*
A: Two things. They both address the same issue, although they come from different perspectives, one of which might be eye-opening and the second of which is just plain terrifying.

The eye-opener first. When you publish a book, everybody you know assumes that your publisher has sent a huge truck of copies for you to give to relatives and friends. The reality is that, by contract, you normally receive only twenty-five free copies of a paperback and the grand total of ten free copies of the hardback. These manage to disappear as soon as they arrive. Mom and Dad, Sis, your best friends, your writing teacher. Bye-bye, books. Of course, you're happy to give them away. What use are they otherwise? But at the end of the day, you're lucky to have a copy for yourself.

If you want more, you need to buy them. To help, your publisher will generously give you a 40 percent discount, the same discount that it gives to most independent book stores. But generosity has its limits. Your publisher will not pay you royalties on the books you buy, even though theoretically there's no difference between buying them at a 40 percent discount and a book store buying them for that discount. In the latter case, you do get a royalty.

So what's to be done about this inequity? Do you blithely buy discounted books from the publisher and forego the royalty, or do you make friends with your local independent book store? Ask to do a signing. Ask the book store for the favor of letting you buy some of the unsold books at its 40 percent discount. The book store isn't hurt. On the contrary, you help its cash flow and save it the cost of shipping back the unsold books. Meanwhile you get a royalty on the books that you bought from the store. Obviously, you're not going to get rich doing this, but in a profession where it's hard to earn a living, buying books this way can make a small difference. Remember that the cost of the books is tax deductible.

Ten free hardbacks—that's the eye opener. Now here's the terror. According to a recent survey about the book business, the average time it takes for a book to go out of print is . . . are you ready? . . . eighteen months. A year and a half. Now you have a book on the market. Now you don't. Thank the IRS for a 1979 ruling in which a power tool company wasn't allowed to depreciate its inventory. The IRS reasoned that metal objects don't disintegrate quickly, so why should the company be allowed a tax depreciation as if its inventory had lost value? The logic for this ruling was soon applied to other companies that didn't have a disintegrating inventory. Such as books. When publishers weren't allowed tax depreciations, they saw no value in storing numerous copies of individual titles for decades as had been the custom. After eighteen months or at most two years, if a book doesn't attract enough buyers to justify the space it occupies, most of its copies are sold for a couple of dollars each to large book outlets who throw them in bins at bargain prices in a process called "remaindering."

By contract, an author usually must be notified if his or her book is about to be remaindered. You have the right to buy as many copies of your books as you want for a couple of dollars each. When your book was first published, you needed copies, so your only choice was to buy them at forty percent off the cover price. Now you're finally getting a bargain. Buy boxes and boxes of your remaindered books. Buy more than you think you'll ever need. Buy hundreds at least. If you can afford it, buy thousands for the simple reason that your publisher isn't going to make any more copies of your book.

What are you going to do with all these books? Follow the

example of Harlan Ellison and Lawrence Block. These guys have been writers for so long that they know every way for a writer to survive. Ellison is renowned for his television scripts ("The City on the Edge of Forever" in the first season of *Star Trek* and several spellbinders, such as "Demon with a Glass Hand," for the original version of *The Outer Limits*) as well as legendary short stories ("I Have No Mouth, and I Must Scream" and "The Whimper of Whipped Dogs"—I love his titles). He wrote novels and various kinds of criticism. He edited anthologies. He won or was nominated for just about every award I can think of. He's a presence.

The same with multiple-award-winner Lawrence Block. He wrote several distinguished series of mystery novels, one of which involves a recovering-alcoholic private detective named Matthew Scudder (*A Ticket to the Bone Yard*). Another series, this one semi-comic, involves a professional thief named Bernie Rhodenbarr, who owns a used-book store in Greenwich Village. The books in this latter series all have "burglar" in the title, as in *The Burglar Who Traded Ted Williams*. They're some of my personal favorites. Block also has two excellent books about writing fiction: *Telling Lies for Fun and Profit* and *Writing the Novel from Plot to Print*.

Follow the example of the pros. When Ellison's and Block's books are remaindered, they buy every copy they can get their hands on. They then wait a few years and sell them as collector's editions, at a price equal to or greater than the cover price. When Ellison gives a lecture, he sells copies of his remaindered books. In his humorous way, he even tells his audience the huge difference between how much he paid for them and how much he's charging for them. The audience loves it. Block has a newsletter in which he tells his fans which remaindered books are now available and at what price. He also sells these books through his website on the Internet. Of course, this tactic works only for big-name authors. But isn't that your hope—to become a best-selling author? If you're just getting started, have faith in yourself and your future. Buy your remaindered books so that you can capitalize on them if you acquire a wide readership.

Last Day of Class

I n 1968, on a remarkable evening and night during my apprenticeship at Penn State, Philip Klass spent eight hours with me,
discussing the strengths and weaknesses of a story I'd written.
He came to the final words, put the pages back in their folder, and
told me, "That's it. That's all I have to teach you." He was exaggerating. Obviously, he knew a lot more about writing. What he
meant was, "There won't be any other marathon sessions." That
proved to be the case. He and I would talk about writing on many
other occasions. But never again would I have so much advice
given to me at one time.

This book is a little like that session, with the difference that I
truly don't have much more to say about writing, although in
other places I addressed this subject. My collection *Black Evening*
has an introduction about writing. It also has a couple of short
stories about writers and their problems. The Warner Books
editions of *First Blood*, *Testament*, *Last Reveille*, *The Totem*, and *The
League of Night and Fog* have introductions that discuss the origins of
those novels and various technical issues about them. For now, let
me conclude with some general remarks.

There are no inferior types of fiction, only inferior practitioners
of them. Back in 1915, Van Wyck Brooks, a noted student of
American culture, wrote "America's Coming-of-Age." In that
influential essay, he deplored the use of "highbrow" and
"lowbrow" as ways of approaching literature. The first, he felt, was
characterized by "the fastidious refinement and aloofness" of the
Genteel Tradition. The second was a product of crass commer-
cialism. In this hierarchy, highbrow authors automatically assumed

that their taste and sensitivity made them superior. Lowbrow authors granted that they were only out to earn a dollar. Brooks condemned both extremes. I agree. If you write something just for the money, don't tell me about it. But if you write something just to prove how precious and smart you are, to make intellectuals think you're important, don't tell me about that, either.

Your goal should be to write something that's important to *you*, not to the critics. Too often, critics are behind the times. In 1851, they so hated *Moby Dick* that Melville never got over their condemnation, predicting that, even if he had written "the Gospels in this century, I should die in the gutter." He wasn't far wrong. While he didn't die in the gutter, he certainly died in obscurity. Only many years later would his books be considered classics.

F. Scott Fitzgerald, so praised in the 1920s, was virtually ignored when his long-delayed *Tender Is the Night* finally appeared in 1934. Prior to his death in 1940, his yearly royalty check from his publisher barely amounted to $33. When he and his companion Sheila Graham went into a Hollywood Boulevard bookstore to look for one of his novels, the clerk said that he'd need to special-order it. Fitzgerald then introduced himself, startling the clerk, who had assumed that Fitzgerald was dead. It wasn't until Arthur Mizener's biography *The Far Side of Paradise* was published in 1951 that Fitzgerald's critical reputation began to be reestablished.

A novel I loved to teach, Kate Chopin's *The Awakening*, appeared in 1899. It portrayed a woman who felt so smothered by her mandarin New Orleans male-dominated culture that she drowned herself. These days, the book is often described as America's *Madame Bovary*, but at the time, critics so disapproved of its feminist theme that Chopin was virtually blacklisted. Not until the 1960s was *The Awakening* recognized as a masterpiece.

Remember what I said about fleeting fame. Forget the critics. The quality of your work should be all that matters to you. Your fiction should be something that only *you* could have written because of your unique background. If it's a Western, fine. I'd love to have written Alan LeMay's *The Searchers*. A romance? By all means. I wish I could have written *Wuthering Heights*. A science-fiction novel? Absolutely. Who wouldn't want to have written Walter M. Miller Jr.'s *A Canticle for Leibowitz*? Horror? I'm in awe of Bram Stoker's *Dracula*. A mainstream novel? I envy E. L. Doctorow for having written *The Book of Daniel*. Indeed, for some writers, mainstream will be the automatic choice because they've been taught it's the only correct one. But don't surrender to the high-brow prejudice that one form is better than another. They are all modes of expression, creative challenges. Some writers fail to blossom because they attempt the kind of fiction that they think they ought to write rather than the kind they want to.

I admire open-minded writers. Consider Graham Greene. Between writing such mainstream novels as *The Power and the Glory*, he gave us classic thrillers, including *This Gun for Hire* and *The Third Man*. (Recently, a highbrow critic made me laugh when he insisted pompously that *This Gun for Hire* was worth reading because it was an indictment of capitalism.) Or look at Jane Smiley. Along with her Pulitzer Prize-winning *A Thousand Acres*, she wrote a suspense thriller, *Duplicate Keys*, and a Western, *The All-True Travels and Adventures of Lidie Newton*.

Not that I recommend hopscotching through various types of fiction. Variety can be stimulating for a writer, but the sad truth is that readers tend to be loyal to a type of fiction rather than to an author. Especially at the start of your career, be consistent. After you choose a type of fiction that appeals to you rather than one you've been told is proper, write it so ambitiously and respectfully that you add to its tradition. If you earn money doing this, congratulations. If you don't, at least you had the satisfaction of creating the story.

My wife, Donna, was once in our front yard when a child from a nearby grade school walked past our house with a folder of his artwork. He asked Donna if she'd like to see some of his paintings. "Sure." So they spread the paintings on the lawn, and the boy explained each of them. "This is the school, and this is the play-ground, and these are my friends." He stared at the paintings for a long time and then shook his head in discouragement. "In my mind, they were a whole lot better."

Isn't that the truth? Every morning, I go to my desk and reread yesterday's pages, only to be discouraged that the prose isn't as good as it seemed during the excitement of composition. In my mind, it was a whole lot better.

Don't give in to doubt. Never be discouraged if your first draft isn't what you thought it would be. Given skill and a story that compels you, muster your determination and make what's on the page closer to what you have in your mind. The chances are you'll never make them identical. That's one of the reasons I'm still hitting the keyboard. Obsessed by the secrets of my past, I try to put metaphorical versions of them on the page, but each time, no matter how honest and hard my effort, what's in my mind hasn't been fully expressed, compelling me to keep trying. To paraphrase a passage from John Barth's "Lost in the Funhouse," I'll die telling stories to myself in the dark. But there's never enough time. There was never enough time.

About the Author

David Morrell is the author of *First Blood*, the award-winning novel in which Rambo was created. He holds a PhD in American literature from the Pennsylvania State University and was a professor in the English department at the University of Iowa until he gave up his tenure to devote himself to a full-time writing career.

"The mild-mannered professor with the bloody-minded visions," as one reviewer called him, Morrell has written numerous best-selling novels that include *The Brotherhood of the Rose* (the basis for a top-rated NBC miniseries), *The Fifth Profession*, and *Extreme Denial* (set in Santa Fe, New Mexico, where he lives). Twenty million copies of his books are in print. His fiction has been translated into twenty-six languages. Visit him at *www.davidmorrell.net.*